Boogⁱ

笑わない

キーポップは

"I am automatic. When I detect adversity approaching, I float to the surface. That's why I am Boogiepop—phantasmal, like bubbles."

遠野 浩平
ouhei Kadono

"*The story of Boogiepop is one that weighs heavily upon me. It's a subject that I still haven't finished sorting out my feelings about.*"

– Takeda Keiji

"I wanted to mess with your mind a bit. Sorry."

– Miyashita Touka

"That was Boogiepop. Ultimately."

– Kirima Nagi

"Now that you have seen me, I cannot allow you to live."

— **Manticore**

"Now, you are our enemy."

— **Saotome Masami**

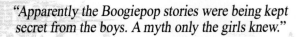

"Apparently the Boogiepop stories were being kept secret from the boys. A myth only the girls knew."

— **Suema Kazuko**

*"I think he loved her
more than I did."*

– Tanaka Shiro

"An alien. He took her with him back into space."

– Kimura Akio

"So, all it ultimately amounts to is nothing?"

– Niitoki Kei

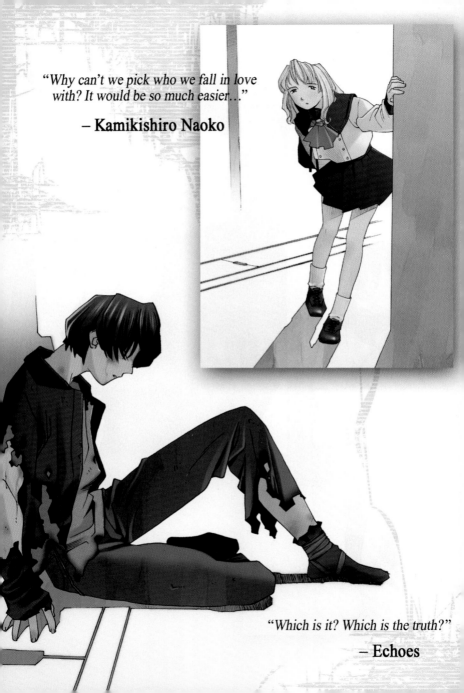

"*Why can't we pick who we fall in love with? It would be so much easier…*"

– Kamikishiro Naoko

"*Which is it? Which is the truth?*"

– Echoes

Boogiepop

and others

Boogiepop
and others

written by
Kouhei Kadono

illustrated by
Kouji Ogata

english translation by
Andrew Cunningham

Seven Seas
LOS ANGELES

BOOGIEPOP AND OTHERS
BOOGIEPOP WA WARAWANAI
© MEDIA WORKS / KOUHEI KADONO 1998
First published in 1998 by Media Works Inc., Tokyo, Japan.
English translation rights arranged with Media Works Inc.

STAFF CREDITS

English Translation: Andrew Cunningham
Layout and Graphic Design: Jon Zamar & Nicky Lim
Assistant Editor: Jason DeAngelis
Editor: Adam Arnold

Publisher: Seven Seas Entertainment

Visit us online at **www.gomanga.com**.

ISBN: 1-933164-16-6

Printed in Canada

First printing: January, 2006

10 9 8 7 6 5 4 3 2 1

table of contents

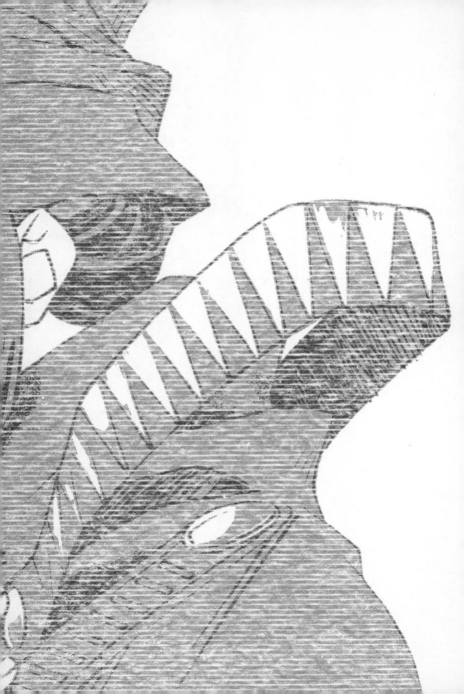

SEVEN SEAS' COMMITMENT TO TRANSLATION AUTHENTICITY

JAPANESE NAME ORDER

To ensure maximum authenticity in Seven Seas' translation of *Boogiepop and Others*, all character names have been kept in their original Japanese name order with family name first and given name second.

For copyright reasons, the names of *Boogiepop* creator Kouhei Kadono and illustrator Kouji Ogata appear in standard English name order.

HONORIFICS

In addition to preserving the original Japanese name order, Seven Seas is committed to ensuring that honorifics—polite speech that indicates a person's status or relationship towards another individual—are retained within this book. Politeness is an integral facet of Japanese culture and we believe that maintaining honorifics in our translations helps bring out the same character nuances as seen in the original work.

The following are some of the more common honorifics you may come across while reading this and other books:

-san – The most common of all honorifics, it is an all-purpose suffix that can be used in any situation where politeness is expected. Generally seen as the equivalent to Mr., Miss, Ms., Mrs., etc.

-sama – This suffix is one level higher than "-san" and is used to confer great respect upon an individual.

-dono – Stemming from the word "tono," meaning "lord," "-dono" signifies an even higher level than "-sama," and confers the utmost respect.

-kun – This suffix is commonly used at the end of boys' names to express either familiarity or endearment. It can also be used when addressing someone younger than oneself or of a lower status.

-chan – Another common honorific. This suffix is mainly used to express endearment towards girls, but can also be used when referring to little boys or even pets. Couples are also known to use the term amongst each other to convey a sense of cuteness and intimacy.

Sempai – This title is used towards one's senior or "superior" in a particular group or organization. "Sempai" is most often used in a school setting, where underclassmen refer to upperclassmen as "sempai," though it is also commonly said by employees when addressing fellow employees who hold seniority in the workplace.

Kouhai – This is the exact opposite of "sempai," and is used to refer to underclassmen in school, junior employees at the workplace, etc.

Sensei – Literally meaning "one who has come before," this title is used for teachers, doctors, or masters of any profession or art.

ブギーポップは笑わない

Boogiepop and Others

Introduction

Opening the *shoji* screen, the boy took a step onto the *tatami* of the darkened tea room.

"........."

Wordlessly, he stared into the center of the room. Cushions and low tables were scattered everywhere.

Only a small amount of light managed to pierce the decorative screen above the door and enter the room, making it difficult to see anything clearly. But he could see the scene easily enough.

In the center of the room was a girl. One look and he knew she was dead.

She was upside-down, thick white cotton socks on slender legs thrust into the air like the arms of a cheerleader at a pep rally. Her shoulders were limp on the floor, her head twisted around so it faced the same direction as her body. There was no blood anywhere.

Her long black hair seemed to flow across the *tatami*, and her vacant eyes just seemed to stare back at the boy.

"........."

The boy took a slow step backwards.

As he did, something hot slid downwards from above, just grazing the tip of his nose.

Startled, he glanced upward towards the ceiling.

He froze.

"You saw me," said the killer hanging from the ceiling. It wore a girl's shape, but was a creature of indeterminate gender. "Now that you have seen me, I cannot allow you to live." Its voice was somewhere between laughing and singing.

A moment later, the boy felt his body flung aside, as the creature lunged down towards him.

"—Gah!"

For some reason, the boy felt oddly happy.

***

…The actual events probably form a very simple story. From a distance, they appear to be quite confusing; to have no clear threads connecting them whatsoever, but the reality is that this is undoubtedly a much more straightforward, commonplace tale.

But from our individual standpoints, none of us were quite able to see the whole picture. All of the people who somehow had a part in this story were unable to see beyond their own unique role.

My name is Niitoki Kei.

I'm in my second year at Shinyo Academy, although I'm so small that I'm often mistaken for a junior high school student, or worse, some elementary school kid. Despite all this, I'm the president of the student discipline committee.

"Kei's like a big sister. She might look like a kid, but there's just something reliable about her," my friends always tell me, half-mockingly.

I don't consider myself to be a particularly serious person, but everyone around me seems to think that I am. They're always asking me for some type of advice or help, and I've got a major sort of glitch where I can't ever seem to tell them no.

"Can you, Kei?"

"Niitoki, please!"

Someone says these words to me and I just can't settle down.

But this has basically nothing to do with me being on the discipline committee.

Our school is only an average, mid-level sort of place, but like many other high schools, it considers guidance to be the teacher's job, and the discipline committee is just there for decoration. It's sad, really. There are a number of students who have run away from home or gone missing this year, but none of the teachers care enough to put forth any effort into finding them, and all the headmaster does is whine about how much of a headache they are, and how poorly they reflect upon the school. Whatever.

All this negligent attitude does is irritate the hell out of me. My tiny little sense of right and wrong is next to useless. It's not like they'll ever listen to me.

If anything of any significance happened to us, we wouldn't be able to do a damn thing about it.

As it was, we knew nothing.

See, all the people close to me, myself included, had no way of knowing each other's problems or just what we were fighting.

We simply had to guess blindly, and just act on our gut.

The man who came from the sky, the woman made from his design—the twisted, strange events they brought about must have begun around that time.

Right as my heart had been broken.

Chapter One
Romantic Warrior

Takeda Keiji
third year, class F

1.

The story of Boogiepop is one that weighs heavily upon me. It's a subject that I still haven't finished sorting out my feelings about.

He's no longer around, but I'm not really sure if I'm supposed to feel relieved about that fact or not.

He was…unusual, to say the least.

I'd never met anyone as strange as him in the seventeen years that I've been alive, and I doubt I ever will again.

After all, he was a transforming super-hero.

That sort of thing is only fun if they're on TV. If you're standing right next to one, it causes nothing but trouble. And, in my case, it wasn't exactly somebody else's problem.

I never once saw him smile.

He always looked grim, and would look at me and say depressing things like, "Takeda-kun, this world is filled with flaws." This, with *the exact same pretty face* that always made my head reel.

But Boogiepop is gone now.

I'll never know if everything he told me was a lie or not.

***

One Sunday, with the middle of fall fast approaching, I was standing in front of the station, waiting for my girlfriend, Miyashita Touka. We were supposed to meet at eleven, but it was already three o'clock, and she had yet to appear.

Did I mention she was a year younger than me? Apparently, her family was pretty strict, and for some stupid reason, I was expressly forbidden from even attempting to call her house. All I could ever do was simply wait for her to get in contact with me. So, once again, I was forced to stand there fretting while I patiently tried to wait for her to show.

"Hey, Takeda-sempai!" someone called out.

I turned around to find Saotome standing there. He was my *kouhai*, on the same committee as I was. There were three other students with him, two of them girls.

"What's this, a double date?" I said, aware that I was coming off as old-fashioned.

"Something like that. You waiting for yours?" Saotome gave off pretty much the same impression whether in uniform or out. Wherever he was, he seemed to blend in. "You do realize that dating's against school rules, right?"

"Look who's talking."

"Oh, you're on the discipline committee as well?" the guy next to Saotome asked.

'Oh, yeah, sorry,' I thought...but I couldn't say that to a *kouhai*, so I just shrugged.

"Then I guess we've got nothing to worry about," he said, putting his arm around the shoulders of the girl next to him.

Guess they were together. Go figure.

"Yeah, I don't give a damn either, but the teachers are a different matter. Better keep an eye out so they don't catch you," I grumbled.

They all gave knowing laughs, then nodded and took their leave. As they walked off, I heard one of the girls say, "Guess who's been dumped!"

All I could think was, 'Mind your own damn business!'

I mean, it's not that I actually like being on the discipline committee. It's just that someone's had to take the job and that someone ended up being me.

That day, Touka never did show.

(Have I really been dumped? Surely there would have been some sort of warning, right?)

I waited despondently until five, unable to let things go.

I knew I had to, though.

I dragged myself away, feeling like the world had cast me aside. I was the only person in my class not going to college. Heck, everyone else was off studying for entrance exams. It's no wonder I felt so left out.

Then it happened.

Staggering towards me was the kind of guy who would stand out in any crowd.

He was a skinny young man, with roughly cropped hair that stood on end. He wore a badly torn, dirty white shirt that was just flung over his body. The shirt was unbuttoned, leaving his bare chest exposed. The bottoms of his pants legs trailed along the ground as his shoeless bare feet shuffled across the pavement.

There was a serious looking wound on his head, and half his face was covered in blood. Though mostly dried, the blood stuck to his hair in clumps. One look at him, and I knew he was a mess, yet I couldn't avert my gaze.

His eyes were unfocused, and he was moaning aloud. This was not some new fashion, but clearly a bona fide, genuinely crazy psychopath. Probably on drugs.

(Yeesh, there are actually guys like this showing up in our town now too…?)

Spooked, I averted my course, giving him a wide berth. Everyone else was doing the same, so there was a sort of air pocket forming around him.

He tottered along in the center for a few moments.

Then, suddenly, he collapsed to the ground.

Before anyone could react, he began to sob quietly.

"Enhhh…enhhhhh…" he sniveled. "Unngghhhhh."

Great, slobby tears rolled down his cheeks, heedless of his surroundings.

A circle of people—myself among them—formed around him, watching. None of us dared move towards him.

It was the strangest thing that I'd ever seen.

It was bizarre, like something out of a surreal Eastern European movie.

But there was one person who did approach him.

He was shorter than me and dressed in a long, black cape with a collar that wrapped around him like a great coat, and a black hat like a shrunken pipe or a top hat without a brim. The hat was a size too big for his head, and half covered his eyes.

On the hat and cape were gleaming bits of metal, like rivets or some sort of badge, sewn along the hem. It gave off the impression of armor.

To match his all-black outfit, he wore black lipstick. His face was so white; it was like the ink painted on top of a glossy *Noh* mask.

Clearly, this was another crazy person on the loose.

The cloaked figure leaned his black hat over to the side, and whispered in the psycho's ear.

The psycho stared up at the cloaked figure with empty eyes.

"......"

The man nodded and the psycho stopped crying.

There was a slight stir from the crowd around them. It seemed that some form of silent communication had been established.

The cloaked figure's face snapped up and glared around at us. It was clear that he was seething with anger.

"Do you think to do nothing when you see a fellow human crying?!" he suddenly shouted, loud and angry, in a clear, boyish soprano voice. "Is this what the advancement of civilization has lead to?! Urban life weeding out and killing the weak?! It's appalling!"

The crowd concluded that he was simply another loony and avoided eye contact, quickly dispersing. I started to follow suit, but he spun towards me, catching my eye. It was then that I finally got a clear look at his face.

Words can't begin to do justice to the shock I felt at that moment.

Perhaps the best example I can give is to describe it like one of those *nopperabou* ghost stories—a faceless ghost, where you expect it to have no face, but instead, it looks just like *you*. At first you just don't get it, but then you do, and it totally freaks you out.

I stared at him, eyes wide open and mouth agape.

But for him, I seemed to be little more than another face in the crowd, and he soon shifted his glare to the man next to me.

Two policemen came rushing up. At last, someone had reported the psycho.

"That him?"

"Get up!"

The policemen roughly tried to yank the man to his feet. He made no attempt to resist.

"No need to be so violent. He's afraid," the black-hatted figure said, not fazed by the idea of lecturing policemen either.

"What are you? His family?"

"Just passing by," the figure replied softly. "Don't twist his arm like that!"

"Step aside!" the policeman shouted, as another tried to shove the cloaked figure away.

But the cloaked figure bent his body like a dancer, and evaded the policeman's sweaty arm.

"Wah!" the policeman cried, overbalancing and falling to his knees.

It was like some kind of kung fu or maybe tai chi. All I know is that the cloaked figure's motions came off as being extremely graceful and fluid.

"This is what happens when you resort to violence," the cloaked figure spat.

"And that's what I call interfering with a police officer!" the cop bellowed, springing to his feet.

"Try performing your duty before you accuse me of interfering with it. It is your job to save people who are in trouble, not to trample them beneath your feet," the cloaked figure said, as if delivering a speech.

Meanwhile, the police had forgotten about the psycho, who had begun aimlessly tottering off down the street again with surprising speed.

The policemen turned hurriedly to give chase, shouting, "Hey, you! Stop right there!"

The cloaked figure in the black hat spun around, his cape fluttering, and dashed away.

"Ah! Wait!" The policemen clearly couldn't decide which quarry to chase.

The cloaked figure moved like the wind, and vanished just as quickly around the next corner.

I was left standing there, stunned.

I was not stunned because of the cloaked figure's bizarre behavior. Well, maybe I was, but much more shocking was having the image of his face burned into my eyes. The hat was low on his face and partially concealed it, but there was no mistaking those big, almond shaped eyes...they belonged to the girl that I had been waiting for all day—Miyashita Touka!

And thus ended my first encounter with the mysterious cloaked figure—Boogiepop.

2.

The next day, I went to school earlier than usual.

The school that I go to, Shinyo Academy, has that *something* a lot of other schools don't. Every student has an ID card, and every time we go in or out of the building, we have to slide it through a gate checker, like one of those ticket readers at the train station. They call it the Campus Advanced Information Administration System (or CAIAS, for short). Supposedly it helps the staff keep track of the exact number of students that attend, since the student population has started to decline as of late.

But in actual practice, it doesn't really change anything. Despite the grand design, this year, there have already been several students who have run away from home, or worse, simply vanished. The system they're so proud of is really powerless when it comes to stopping students from doing whatever they like once they're off school grounds. It's what free will is all about.

Anyway, our school is up in the mountains, so we have to walk up long, steep, green roads just to get there. On this particular morning, there was hardly anybody out on the road.

The sports teams had long since started morning practice, but the rest of the student body had not yet started to arrive.

"Yoohoo! *Keiji!!*" came a cheerful girl's voice from behind.

I turned around to find a girl from my class, Kamikishiro Naoko, walking towards me.

This girl had a habit of over-pronouncing people's names, like she was sight-reading a word in some other language. Plus, she was always chirpy.

"Now, now. Why so gloomy on such a *beautiful* morning?" she said, running to catch up, and thumping me hard on the back.

Both Kamikishiro and I were breaking the school rules against dating. You could say that it gave us a certain connection; a certain ease to our interaction. A sort of sympathy that we couldn't expect to get from friends of the same gender. We always joked around together, but today I was hardly in the mood.

"You're early," I said curtly. "Not going for your usual dramatic entrance?"

Kamikishiro was almost compulsively late and she always insisted that it was due to low blood pressure. If a teacher tried to chew her out for it, she would apologize dramatically and quite flirtatiously, I might add, which generally left the male teachers flustered, but it always seemed to do the trick, getting her off the hook. A powerful technique, indeed.

"Yeah, well, had some stuff to take care of today. But spill already! How was your date yesterday?"

"F-forget about it."

"You have a fight or something?" she asked, peering closely at my face with interest. She had a tendency to express her emotions a bit too obviously. She was very pretty, but had an open, loud laugh. This seemed to make some people think badly of her, no matter how good a person she was at heart.

"A fight? I wish we could have," I sighed.

"Wait, what? That sounds serious!"

"Whatever."

Another student passed us on a bicycle, so we fell quiet.

As always, there was a committee member posted at the gates, like a train station guard, making sure the cards went through the gate check smoothly.

"Oh, Takeda-sempai, you're early," said today's guard, Niitoki Kei. She was the discipline committee president. Despite the ominous title, she was a tiny, cute girl with a childish face.

"D-ditto," I said, waving. We'd been on the health board together last year as well, so we had seen each other regularly for two years.

"Mornin', *Kei*!" said Kamikishiro. Although they were friends already, Niitoki had ignored Kamikishiro's dates on several occasions, and this had brought them even closer together.

"My, my, are you two *together* now?" Niitoki said, eyes wide.

"That's scary, coming from you," Kamikishiro laughed.

"I didn't mean it that way, really. Even if it were true, my lips are sealed."

"Trying to earn a favor, eh? Looks expensive."

"It is," the committee president laughed.

If she knew that Kamikishiro had both a second and first year student in her saddle, I doubt she could have been so blasé about it. She was pretty serious, and she would probably get so angry that steam would shoot out of her ears.

We put our cards through the gate check and went inside.

"Sempai, don't forget the meeting today!" she said as I waved in acknowledgement.

Kamikishiro giggled. "She's so cute."

"Who?"

"*Kei*. You know she's got a crush on you, right? Puppy love…"

"You're one to talk."

Every relationship she had ended up like a war zone. I'm amazed she could still joke about it.

"So what was it? *Fuji-chan* dump you?" Who knows why Kamikishiro always called Touka by a different reading of the *kanji* in her name, but here she was doing it again.

"She stood me up."

"I can see why you got chest pains then! Ah ha ha!!"

I suspected that she, too, stood up many a man.

"What are girls thinking when they do that?" I asked. "It sure as hell isn't about their boyfriend."

"That's not an easy thing to answer. Hmm…it all depends, really. I know that it's not always because they don't want to see you, though. You know, stuff just sort of comes up."

"So what if they stand you up and dress like a man?"

"Hunh? What are you talking about?! What's that supposed to mean?" Kamikishiro's eyes widened.

Understandably. I didn't know the answer either.

"Never mind. Must have been seeing things."

"I don't really get it…but you've got a lot of time on your hands, so you really ought to start taking love more seriously, ya hear?" she said in a sing-song voice.

"What?" I replied, scowling, and she burst into song.

"Life is brief, young maiden, fall in love;

before the crimson bloom fades from your lips,
before the tides of passion cool within your hips,
for those of you who know no tomorrow."

"You're in a good mood. You in love *again*?"

"Kinda. Tee hee hee."

"For crying out loud, how many is this now?"

Before we hit the halls, we smoothly shifted to a more standoffish attitude. We weren't going out, but it was never a good idea to start any rumors.

I let my feet carry me to Touka's class.

Once there, it wasn't like I could actually talk to her, so I wasn't exactly sure why I was going, but I couldn't seem to help myself.

Touka's room was year two, class C, and it was still empty.

Feeling suddenly tired, I flopped down on a chair inside.

Once again the cloaked figure's words ran through my mind, *'Do you think to do nothing when you see a fellow human crying?!'*

I paused for a moment.

Was that *really* Touka?

A twin brother, perhaps…?

No, she'd never mentioned one before.

I heard someone coming, so I quickly got up and left the room.

I stood as inconspicuously as I could in the covered passage, a few yards away from the room, and kept watch. The more I watched, the more pathetic I felt.

(Aw, hell…)

Touka was about the twentieth student to arrive.

She was the same as always. There was no sign of any strange hat.

But for some reason, she had an enormous Spalding bag in addition to her usual school bag. The sort that people generally keep sneakers or gym clothes in.

Then she noticed me.

She shot me a quizzical, innocent glance.

I found myself grinning and nodding.

She smiled softly and nodded back.

Nothing different than usual.

She didn't seem at all bothered about having stood me up either.

So as not to get noticed, we hardly ever spoke to each other at school. But words weren't necessary. We had worked out our own sort of sign language that only the two of us knew.

So I made one of those signs, putting my index finger up. This sign meant back of the garden after school.

She made the same gesture, showing consent.

Yeah, it was just like nothing had happened.

Feeling like I was surrounded by a heavy smoke cloud, I drifted back to my own classroom.

Kamikishiro wasn't there yet. Probably still 'taking care of stuff.' Same as me.

***

The discipline committee meeting was during lunch.

"Ehem, I expect that all of you have noticed, but this year, discipline has become rather slack. There are now four girls, students here, who appear to have run away."

They called it a meeting, but we hardly ever spoke at all. The teacher in charge would be the one to drone on and on at us the whole time.

Frankly, we may have been called the discipline committee, but not one of us was operating under the illusion we could actually control anybody. Most of us were, like me, breaking those rules ourselves.

The boy I met in town yesterday, Saotome, was the secretary. He took minutes in a notebook. Despite double dating on the side, he melted right into the atmosphere here, like a model committee member.

"If any of you happen to hear about anything like that, then please, come running to me. One of their friends might be able to get in touch with them."

We made no response. We never did. The teacher never seemed to notice.

"Incidentally, the infamous Kirima Nagi failed to arrive this morning. Make sure to keep an eye on her, hear? No telling what that girl's plotting in the shadows."

He glanced sharply around the room.

We remained silent.

The only sound was the scritching of Saotome's pen, jotting down absurdly complete minutes.

Suddenly, the PA system crackled to life.

"…Miyashita Touka, second year, class C. Please, return to the infirmary at once. Miyashita Touka, second year, class C…"

I jerked in my seat, and it made a screeching sound on the floor.

"Mm? Something the matter?" The teacher glared at me balefully.

"I, uh, feel dizzy," I said to excuse my actions, but in fact my head was reeling.

"Are you okay, *sempai*?" the president asked. "You look pale."

"Third year? You go on back to class."

Seniors had exams to study for and didn't really play a major role on the committee. Heck, they didn't even need to come the meetings in the first place. Of course, I wasn't taking exams, but the teacher hadn't bothered to remember that, apparently.

"Okay."

I stood up, and the president followed suit.

"Sensei, I'll take him to the infirmary."

The teacher made a face, but then simply ordered her to hurry back.

"…That okay?" I asked Niitoki.

"Are *you* okay?" she whispered back.

I said nothing else, but rushed to the infirmary.

There was no one there.

I let out a huge sigh of relief.

The announcement had asked Touka to 'return,' so she must have been there before, but gone out again.

(No, she was supposed to go home, but she must still be on campus. Her card hasn't been swiped through the gate…)

Thinking furiously, I slumped down on the bench beside me.

"…You're worried about her?" Niitoki asked.

"Yeah, a little."

I looked up, and she spoke quickly, stiffly, "I thought as much. I'm in the same class as her."

I gaped at her, but she kept talking.

"She's been a little off recently. Like she can't sit still. Glaring outside during class. The teacher yells at her about it a lot. I thought she might be having trouble with you or something."

I had no answer.

"I like you too, you know. But—"

"………"

"But it looks like you like her more than me."

She was glaring at me now.

I couldn't think of any way to respond.

"I'm going back now," she snapped, and bolted out of the infirmary.

Needless to say, I was out of it for pretty much the rest of the day.

***

After class, I went to the place where we had agreed to meet, but Touka wasn't there.

Sunlight barely filtered down to the deserted rear of the building, so it was quite dark around me.

I threw my bag on the ground, shoved my hands in my pockets, and leaned against the wall.

I couldn't figure out what to do next, so I stared aimlessly up at the sky.

The edge of the school roof made a clear straight line cutting the sky in half.

But there was a shadow jutting over that line.

I gasped in shock.

It was the silhouette of a person. A person with a flat, pipe-like protrusion on their head, wrapped in what seemed like a cape.

At that moment, I knew it was him. It was the mysterious cloaked figure.

When he saw me, he spun around and pulled away.

I yelled towards him, "W-wait!"

Right beside me, there was an old fire escape. It was connected to windows on each floor and went all the way to the roof.

I vaulted the locked gate at the bottom and raced up the stairs to the roof—in clear violation of school policy.

When I hit the roof, I yelled, "Miyashita! That you?!"

The cloaked figure slowly emerged from the shadows. He stared directly at me again.

"You...know Miyashita Touka?" he said in Touka's voice. It was a little deeper, more male sounding, but if you listened for it, it was clearly hers. "I see. We met yesterday, didn't we? I have done you wrong. I ignored you, and for that...I apologize."

I rushed over to him and grabbed him by the shoulders.

"What the hell are you talking about?!"

Suddenly, my body was wafting through the air, and then came crashing down upon the concrete with a hard thud.

"_____?!"

Had he swept my legs out from under me? The pain raced through my entire body before I figured it out.

"What...what's going on?" I cried.

"I should state clearly that I am not Miyashita Touka. Currently, I am Boogiepop," the cloaked figure whispered.

"C-currently?"

So, it had been her this morning? Is that what he meant?

"I'm sure you've heard the idea before. Simply put, it

resembles the concept of the split personality. Understand me so far?" this 'Boogiepop' continued.

"S-split—?"

"None of you have noticed yet, but danger is hovering above this school…and all mankind. That is why I have emerged."

I couldn't quite decide if I really should be referring to Boogiepop as 'he' or not, but I could tell from his expression that he was deadly serious.

3.

That evening, I called Touka's house directly.

"Miyashita speaking," her mother answered.

In my most serious voice, I said, "Hello. This is Takeda from the Shinyo Academy discipline committee. Is Touka present?"

When she heard the words 'discipline committee,' Touka's mother made a little gasping sound into the receiver.

"H-has Touka done anything…? But we haven't seen *that* since she started high school…"

That?

"I'd like to speak to her directly, if possible."

"O-of course! Just a moment," she said in a much too respectful tone for some high school kid. Any other mother would have just said, "Hang on a sec," or something equally trite. She must have been distressed.

"Touka speaking," said Touka, in her usual voice.

"Hi, it's Takeda."

"Yes?" she said flatly. Presumably her mother was

hovering near by.

Apparently, the Miyashita residence still didn't have any other extensions.

"Did you go somewhere this Sunday?"

"Not really," she said, knocking the receiver twice. I took this to mean the same as two fingers held up in our sign language. It meant, 'Sorry, not right now.'

Obviously, I already knew that, but I had to ask anyway.

"Hey."

"Yes?"

"You ever heard of Boogiepop?"

"Eh?" she said blankly. I'd caught her completely off guard. "What's that?" She wasn't acting. She really didn't know.

"Never mind. It's not important. I just really wanted to hear your voice, is all. Sorry."

"Thank you," she said, very politely as if for her mother's benefit. I translated it as a sign of pleasure.

So, it looked like she didn't hate me after all.

"Then I'll see you tomorrow at school."

"Sounds good."

I hung up first, and silence overcame me.

I crossed my arms and tried to think. That Boogiepop guy had been right. Touka had completely forgotten about our date on the day before, and our promise to meet after school today.

"She doesn't know," he had said, standing on the school roof, in the light of the setting sun. "If something threatens to erode her foothold of ignorance, she instantly ceases to know that as well. To erase the anomaly caused by not meeting you yesterday, she will have deleted all memories of the date from her mind."

"Deleted?" I said, still reeling, barely keeping up. "You mean, she's forgotten that we were supposed to meet?"

"Precisely. But this is assuredly not because she doesn't take you seriously. Quite the reverse. I imagine she loves you quite a lot. Which is exactly why she needs to forget so thoroughly."

"How so?"

"So that she doesn't feel guilty. She doesn't want to even think about you being mad at her. But *that* is something beyond her control," he said from her very own lips.

"What exactly *are* you? How long have you been... possessing her?"

"Possessing? Can't say I like that choice of words. It's not like I chose to appear."

"Then why do you?!"

"Because danger is upon us," he said, gazing at me levelly.

I flinched. His gaze held daggers.

"I am automatic. When I detect adversity approaching, I float up out of Miyashita Touka. That's why I am Boogiepop—phantasmal, like bubbles."

"Adversity? What kind of...?"

"There is a devil nesting in this school."

I know that sounds absolutely nuts coming from me, but when he said it, the look in his eyes was unmistakable—he was completely serious.

The setting sun sent long shadows across the roof. Boogiepop's black clothes made him look half invisible and he virtually faded into the darkness.

"It's hidden among you now, but it poses a very real threat. It has barely begun to stir, but once it does, it will mean the end of the world."

His words were the ravings of a lunatic, but if you actually looked at him and heard his voice, they were horribly convincing.

"Are…aren't you the same thing?" I asked, resisting him with everything I had. For me, this man taking up residence in Touka's body was pretty much the same as the end of the world.

Touka's other personality replied calmly, "I'm aware of that, which is why I never come out for long. This is also automatic. The rest of the time, I live peacefully as Miyashita Touka; gazing at you with ardor."

"Ardor? Hey…!"

There was something antiquated about his manner of speaking. He even called me *'kimi,'* like a scholar from the Meiji era.

"My time today will shortly end. There is little meaning in my keeping watch like this, once school is over. Everyone has already gone home."

"…So this dangerous being you've been going on about is one of the students?" I found myself asking.

Boogiepop nodded, "Most likely."

"What is it, exactly?"

"It is better if you don't know."

"Why?"

"Because it is too dangerous. If you know more, something might happen to you. I would prefer to keep Miyashita Touka's lover out of harm's way."

I know I'm repeating myself, but he really does keep saying this with her face and her voice.

"If it's that dangerous, I think I should know. That body doesn't belong to you alone, you know." Even as I spoke, part of me was arguing that I shouldn't take this guy seriously. Clearly, this was all just a paranoid delusion, caused by some bizarre psychological disease, brought about by an instability in Touka's mind...yet the creature before me was Touka and not Touka at the same time. I couldn't think otherwise.

Boogiepop sighed. "All right, but don't tell anyone else."

"Right," I replied, swallowing hard. I steeled myself for anything.

But his words were too simple, and caught me by surprise. "It's a man-eater."

***

After I called Touka's house, I slumped dejectedly on my bed.

My head was a mess.

A split personality?

The school...no, the entire world was in danger?

What the hell?!

As delusions went, it was pretty damn delusional. It was like one of those crazy school-bound RPGs.

(But I don't want to exactly go and drag Touka off to some psych ward...)

Boogiepop had said Touka forgets everything. So, in a worst-case scenario, even if we went to a hospital and had a doctor look at her, Boogiepop might never even appear. That would make her seem like the sane one, while whoever took her would come off looking like a complete idiot.

On the way home from school, I had bought a paperback called *The Scream Inside - Multiple Personality Disorder*, so I decided to delve into it now. I'd just grabbed the easiest looking one, but to my surprise, there had been an entire section in the bookstore on psychological disorders. Surely, the world was crazy enough already without all these diseases, I thought.

The writer wrote in a very conversational tone, so it was readable enough, but the sentences were filled with difficult words that left my head spinning. I did catch the phrase, "This disease is exceedingly rare—if not almost unheard of—in Japan."

As far as I could tell, multiple personality disorder generally arises when someone is trapped in an oppressive situation and unable to cope with reality, shifting their emotions onto another personality in an attempt to create a new life. "The human psyche is open to the possibilities of both good and evil. In my opinion, multiple personality disorder occurs when one of these possibilities, suppressed by societal pressures, declares independence and begins to fight to exist. Regardless of how diseased the result or how destructive it is on the host body and those around it, the possibility makes no distinction between good or evil." There was a lot of stuff like this where I kind of understood what I was reading, but at the same time, I didn't. Apparently in Japan, the basis for this type of action usually didn't have a clear form, which meant that the vast majority of incidents would result in schizophrenia rather than multiple personality disorder. To me, it's like talking about the difference between 'God' and 'The Universe.'

The author's name was Kirima Seiichi. There wasn't an author's profile attached to the book, so I had no way of telling who he was or what his credentials were. But somehow, what I'd read just felt right.

(Then what sort of possibility was Boogiepop? What had suppressed him?)

I flopped back onto bed and stared at the ceiling.

Do you think to do nothing when you see a fellow human

crying?!'

Those words rang through my head again. For some reason, I just couldn't stop thinking about them.

***

"...So that's what it said. What do you think?" I asked Boogiepop. It was the next day after school, and we were both on the roof again.

"A suppressed possibility? Hmm...not a bad explanation, I suppose."

Miyashita had not been in class, so I'd swung by the roof on the off chance he was around. It seemed as though he took over the moment classes ended.

"But, in my case, I am not one of Miyashita Touka's other possibilities."

"Then what are you?"

"Good question. This world's...?" he said quite naturally.

For a moment, I couldn't grasp his meaning. It felt as though he hadn't finished his sentence, but, instead, had just let it trail off. 'This world's...?' This world's *what*?

Ignoring my blank look, he forged on, "I have no autonomy. I have no idea what Miyashita Touka might be thinking. She may well have some possibility, some hidden desire that produced me. But that has nothing to do with me. I have no dreams. I have only my duty. I am here only to carry out my purpose."

"To save mankind?"

"Yes."

"Why you?"

"I do not know. I would like to," Boogiepop sighed,

staring up at the sky above his head.

Not looking at me, he continued, "So you wish to 'cure' me then?"

I jumped. Of course, part of me did want to. Miyashita Touka was my girlfriend. But I also felt it wasn't something that I *had* to do.

"Mm, no…I dunno."

I wasn't making a guarded answer to keep an eye on his reaction; I was genuinely not sure any more. It didn't seem like his presence was hurting anyone. Touka herself remained blissfully unaware.

(Only thing it actually interferes with is our dates.)

"I admit it would be better if I did not exist. If only there were no need for me…"

His profile was exactly like that of the girl I loved, and it looked somehow forlorn, so without thinking, I blurted out, "It must be hard for you…"

Not exactly the way you react to the ravings of a delusional multiple personality, I admit.

"Well, I'm hardly ever here, so…"

I'd thought he might be angered by my awkward attempt at sympathy, but he responded quietly. Not crazy at all.

The two of us looked up at the sky. It was cloudy. This time, there was no beautiful sunset…only darkness. There was a chill in the air, and it seemed as though cold rain might start falling at any second. It was the kind of day that dampens your spirit.

"Can I ask you something?"

"What's that?"

"The first time I saw you, what did you say to that homeless guy?"

"Nothing important."

"How did you make him stop crying?"

"I just gave him the encouragement he needed. Every person needs help when they're suffering."

"He needed help? How did you know?"

"He was crying. You could tell he was suffering just by looking at him," he said plainly, like it was the most obvious thing in the world.

"But…but…" I sputtered, then sighed. "The rest of us ordinary people can't understand that way of thinking." Even as I said it, I felt pathetic.

"You're a good man," Boogiepop suddenly said.

"Huh?"

"I think I know what Miyashita Touka sees in you."

"Please don't say things like that with her face. When I meet her tomorrow, I won't know what to do…" I said, realizing that this meant I had completely accepted Boogiepop as an independent existence.

Boogiepop made a strange expression. Beneath the low brim of his hat, his left eye narrowed and the right side of his mouth twisted upwards. It was a very asymmetrical expression that Touka herself would never make.

"Don't worry. I am me, and she is herself."

Later, I wondered if that expression was a strained sort of grin, but at the time, it baffled me. It was a sort of grin that seemed both sarcastic and somewhat diabolical at the same time.

I never did see him smile, though.

4.

After that, it became routine to join Boogiepop on the roof every day as he 'kept watch.'

"I'm not really part of my class anymore," I complained to him.

"You aren't taking exams?"

"No, my father knows someone who owns a design firm, so I've been working there part time. He said that I had good sense and that I shouldn't bother with college. That I'd be better off just starting to work for him directly."

"The boss' favorite craftsman, then."

Touka had once said, "Are you sure? Sounds risky to me…" but Boogiepop sounded impressed.

Happily, I enthused, "Exactly, a craftsman. That's what a designer is, really. We make what we've been asked to make."

"Seems like you've got both feet on the ground," Boogiepop said, sounding almost jealous. He lived half in some unearthly realm that only he could see.

"But Miyashita thinks it sounds dangerous."

"She would. I don't know her all that well, but there are far more girls who shun romantic men than there are those who are attracted to them."

"Really? I mean, romantic?" It was an embarrassing word.

"I have no such hopes, but I believe humans need some sort of dream. Am I wrong?" Boogiepop always looked especially serious when he said things like this.

"I dunno," I muttered.

"When you have no dream, when you can't imagine a future, that means something in this world is flawed. Unfortunately, it is not I who will battle that flaw, but you and Miyashita Touka," the self-described defender of the world said, staring into the distance.

Based only on his words, and on his outfit, it was impossible to think of him as anything but a clown. After all, he had a woman's face, but he talked like a man.

But I thought if he was a clown, then I wanted to be a clown too.

***

Being with him, talking with him, I could see no traces of Touka anywhere. What had happened to her to make him appear?

"When did you first come out?" I asked, one day.

"About five years ago. Miyashita's parents were fighting, considering divorce. Her uncertain feelings at the time may have produced a stubborn creature like me. But I, myself, was far too busy fighting a killer that was stalking the streets to really pay much attention."

I had a hunch which killer he was talking about. Five years

ago, a serial killer had murdered five girls, and hung himself when it seemed they were about to catch him. It was a very well-known story, so it made sense for it to be incorporated into his delusion.

"Miyashita's mother sounded like she knew about you…"

"Mm, she's seen me a few times. We're talking back in Junior High, after all. Miyashita Touka was not exactly free to move around. She even caught me climbing out the window once."

"Must have been surprised."

"She was hysterical, which caused me no end of trouble. She locked me in the house, so I had to knock the woman out to make my escape. Danger was approaching, after all."

"Seriously?" No wonder her mother was freaked. It also explained why the Miyashita household didn't let her have a phone in her room.

"After that, I suspect Miyashita Touka was dragged off to a psychologist, but I can only speculate. I never appeared."

"She didn't show any…unusual signs?"

Since the condition was almost unheard of in Japan, the doctor probably didn't believe a word of it.

"Probably not. I imagine they had their doubts about the mother, though. After all, they were having marital problems at the time. But apparently, the whole fuss caused her father to blame himself and make amends. Things settled down after that."

"Hmmm…" This reminded me of something from the book I'd read. Not a multiple personality case, but a manic-depressive girl. At school, she never spoke a word to anyone, but she was always bright and happy at home. Her parents and grandparents were apathetic and cold, and she desperately tried to brighten up the gloomy atmosphere. Unfortunately, the stress was too much for her, and its effects started to manifest externally. Her behavior grew stranger and stranger, until finally she was taken to a doctor and the truth came out. She was treated, her family repented, and the house became a much more peaceful place. This sort of "peace making" psychological disorder is apparently referred to as "the Trickster."

For some reason, it sounded a lot like Boogiepop to me.

"So," I said, and explained all this to him.

He made that strange expression again. "Miyashita Touka may well see it that way."

"But you're still here, even though that situation is over. Why? You never come out at home any more, right?"

"Right."

"Then why?"

"I can't explain it. I simply have my duty to fulfill."

"You'll just disappear when this 'danger' is over?"

"Yes. I will be a little sad to go this time, though. I won't be able to see you again."

This surprised me.

"You won't…?"

"Right. Miyashita Touka will be here, of course. I imagine you prefer her," his shoulders slumped a little.

I couldn't think of anything to say, so I remained silent.

The two of us stared quietly up at the evening sky.

Boogiepop began to whistle. The tune was fast and bright, his breathing skillfully alternating fast and slow, but it was a whistle, so it sounded rather sad somehow.

I remembered that Touka couldn't whistle.

(A suppressed possibility…?)

Even as her boyfriend, I suppose I was suppressing some part of her.

This thought weighed heavily on me.

He finished whistling, and I applauded. "You're good. What song is that?"

"Overture to the first act of "Die Meistersinger von Nurnberg.""

"Of what?"

"The most flamboyant piece this noisily, romantic, old composer Wagner ever wrote."

"Classical? Hunh. Thought it was rock…"

"You'd have preferred "Atom Heart Mother"? I tend to like the old music," he said, narrowing one eye.

All of our twilight ramblings passed in this fashion.

5.

One day, Kamikishiro was gone. She just stopped coming to school.

I didn't know much, but it seemed that she had run away.

"You're kidding?" I said as I heard the news.

"Really! The teacher told us. She hasn't come home," one of the girls in class said calmly.

"Why? Why would she run away?"

"I don't know. That girl hardly ever talked to us. I bet she thought her pretty face would let her get by in Tokyo or something," the girl snorted.

The girls in class were much less expressive than Kamikishiro, who was always laughing and joking.

"B-but...she had good grades. She looked like she was ready to pass the entrance exam for the college that she wanted to go to, right?"

"You sure know a lot about her."

"What, did you have a thing for her, Takeda-kun?"

"It's not like that. Still..." I started to say.

The leader of the girls in class, Sasaki, said quietly, "I think I know how she felt. Ultimately, she just wanted to escape."

"Escape? From what?" I asked, surprised. Kamikishiro had two boyfriends, one a first year, one in second year. I wondered if she was escaping them.

But Sasaki meant something else. "You wouldn't understand, Takeda-kun."

"Why not?"

"Because you don't have exams. How could you possibly understand the pressure?"

I had no defense against that argument.

"Right, you can't understand."

"Yeah, yeah."

The other girls joined in, almost accusatory.

The other students weren't watching us directly, but they weren't not watching, either. They just sort of sat around us, flipping through their vocabulary flashcards.

"I'd run away if I could. But I can't. We're not as irresponsible as Kamikishiro," Sasaki said very coldly.

Everyone nodded.

Not one of them appeared to be the least bit worried about her.

"...*When you see a fellow human crying,*" I heard Boogiepop's voice whisper in my ear.

The teacher arrived. We stopped talking and went back to our seats.

I could barely manage to sit through class.

The guy in front of me was studying something else. Everyone was only in class for their transcripts; all of them were certain that their test scores were far more important than learning itself. Even the teachers agreed, so they just lectured tediously, never calling on anyone, never asking if there were any questions.

Why the hell were we even here?

What had happened to Kamikishiro? Had her cheery exterior been a lie? I thought it was sometimes, but I didn't think she was the sort of girl to just up and run away.

"For those of you who know no tomorrow."

But even so, I was just like the people around me. I knew nothing.

I hadn't even known that Touka was possessed by this Boogiepop guy.

I didn't listen to the teacher for the rest of class, and I sure as hell didn't take any notes. For all my complaints, I was even less serious about this than the people taking exams. Without any purpose, I just sat there stewing.

***

That day, Boogiepop wasn't waiting on the roof.

"…………"

I waited for him a while, but eventually the sun set, and I had to give up and go home.

***

When I climbed up to the roof the next day, Boogiepop was waiting for me, but this time in a girl's school uniform; no strange costume.

"Hey," he said, raising his hand. This gesture is how I knew it was him. Otherwise, I would have taken him for Touka.

"No costume?"

"Don't need it any more. So she didn't bring it with her."

He had explained once before that Touka would unconsciously carry it around with her, but I hadn't ever thought anything of it until now.

"What do you mean?"

"The danger is over," he said flatly.

"Eh?"

"Everything's finished, Takeda-kun."

"W-wait! That's so…"

"That's all there is to it. That's the way I'm made. When the danger is gone, I disappear. Like bubbles."

"The danger…weren't you going to save the world? It hasn't been saved at all!"

"But my job is finished. What you mean by 'save' is not my job," he said, shaking his head quietly.

"But you said you were going to fight the devil that lives in this school!"

"I did. I'm not the one that killed it, though…"

My mouth flapped wordlessly. I couldn't think of anything else to say. "But…but…that's…"

"Thank you, Takeda-kun," Boogiepop suddenly bowed his head. "I enjoyed my time with you. Until now, I had never done anything but fight. You're the first person I could really call a friend. Perhaps you only spent time with me because I'm part of Miyashita Touka, but I had fun. I mean it."

"………"

I suddenly realized just how much I liked him.

I'd liked him since we first met in town.

And not because he had Touka's face.

Everything I wanted to say but couldn't express…he could and would at the drop of a hat. That's why I liked him so much.

"Don't go."

"Eh?"

"Don't go anywhere. You're about the only friend I have. I'd really like to keep meeting you," I hung my head, almost whispering. I may have been crying.

Boogiepop made that face again.

"That's not true, Takeda-kun."

"It is!"

"You simply aren't connecting with the world around you right now."

I stopped breathing.

"Miyashita Touka's worried about you too. Don't let yourself think you're the only one who's worried."

"But…but what about you? If you just vanished without anyone the wiser, doesn't that make you sad?"

"You're the wiser, aren't you?"

"But I'm…"

"I'm afraid you and Miyashita Touka have your job to do, just as I have my duty. You two have to make your own world. You don't have time to waste belittling yourself," Boogiepop said curtly.

There was nothing left for me to say. I hung my head and stuttered, "B-but…"

When I looked up…there was nobody there.

Startled, I raced across the roof.

But there was no sign of him anywhere.

Just like the first time I saw him, he'd vanished in the wind.

***

When I came down the fire escape, I found Miyashita waiting for me at the bottom.

I could tell instantly that it wasn't him. When she looked at me, she smiled.

"You're late, Takeda-sempai!" she said, in a voice that seemed to tumble.

"Eh…"

"You told me to wait here? And then you show up late, you big meany."

I was taken aback. Then, it hit me.

'She doesn't know anything.'

'She doesn't even notice that she doesn't know. Her memories are automatically corrected.'

That explained it.

She had automatically created a reason for her to be here.

"Ah, uh…s-sorry. I bumped into a friend."

"On the roof? Were you called out by the school thugs?"

"Does our school even have any?"

"Good point," she laughed.

Suddenly, I felt a great affection for her. "You got cram school today?"

"Yeah, at five."

"I'll walk you to the station."

She looked surprised. "Leave school together?"

"Hey, I'm on the discipline committee."

"You sure?"

"The gate guards are all my *kouhai*. They'll let us by."

I didn't let her squirm out of it, but we didn't hold hands or anything.

Niitoki was watching the gate. For some reason, the school's problem child, Kirima Nagi, fresh off from suspension the previous Friday, was standing next to her.

She was slim and tall, and all the guys said she was as pretty as a model, but she looked a little harsh to me.

She was the polar opposite of Niitoki, and I was surprised to see them acting so friendly towards one another. When they stood next to each other, they looked like sisters with years between them, or perhaps a mother and child who were closer in age.

"Oh, *sempai*," Niitoki said, smiling despite seeing her classmate Touka standing next to me.

"Hey," I grunted.

"Hmm. So, you're Miyashita Touka," said Kirima Nagi abruptly, suddenly standing right in front of her.

"Y-yes…"

"I'm Kirima. Nice to meet you," she said, thrusting out her hand. She sounded more like a man.

"Hey!" I said, butting in, but Touka bobbed her head and took the offered hand.

Kirima Nagi made a wry smile that reminded me of Boogiepop, and walked on by.

While we were still stunned, Niitoki said, "Come on now, *sempai,* Miyashita-san. Run your cards through."

We did as we were told and exited the school.

The road was covered in fallen leaves.

"These maple leaves look so beautiful when they're falling, but once they've fallen, they're just a mess," Touka said, walking carefully to avoid getting them stuck to her shoes.

"Mm, but they're still lovely when they fall."

"That your opinion as a designer?"

"Not really."

"I'm jealous of you, you know," Touka pouted as she suddenly started stomping through the leaves.

"H-hey…"

"I've got to take a quiz on idioms today. I hate it." The leaves squelched beneath her feet as if she were tap dancing.

"You say that, but—"

"But I'm still going to college," she interrupted, still keeping her face turned away from mine, slopping through the leaves. "No matter what you say."

"What I say?" I couldn't remember saying anything against it.

"You went and decided what you were going to do all by yourself. You're all confident now. Like you're snickering at the rest of us."

"That's what…" I was about to say, 'Everyone else was doing,' but she looked up at me seriously, and I bit my tongue.

"That was pretty stressful, you know. I thought it was going to eat me alive. But I'm over that now. Finished with it."

She looked up.

I was surprised.

She looked just like Boogiepop.

"To tell you the truth, *sempai*, I remember standing you up that Sunday."

"Eh?"

"But I wanted to mess with your mind a bit. Sorry," she said, and bowed her head.

Her movements were Touka's. There was no hint of

Boogiepop.

(It can't be…)

Her anxiety had called out Boogiepop?

Was that the 'devil in the school?'

Does that mean—that I had defeated it?

She had told me of her worries through Boogiepop, and she no longer needed to be afraid. The 'danger' had passed.

I stopped in my tracks. My eyes were wide. Touka was staring at her shoes. "They're all dirty now," she said.

She giggled then, sheepishly.

Boogiepop had said he had no dreams. He never laughed. "Eh heh heh."

I looked at Touka's pretty, cheerful smile, and thought, Boogiepop can't do *that*.

It's our job to laugh.

Interlude

Somewhere between day and night, in a dim, gloomy room, a girl lay on her side, without a stitch of clothing on her. She wasn't moving.

The Manticore stood next to her.

The room was silent.

Slowly, elegantly, it stooped over the fallen girl.

It brushed aside the girl's hair, and kissed her on the forehead.

It moved down to her nose, then her chin, neck, chest, stomach, and abdomen, licking each of them, leaving a thin blue trail. Everywhere its saliva touched changed color.

When it had licked the girl all over, the Manticore moved its mouth away.

The girl's body began to change.

All over the surface of her skin, snap, snap, thin cracks tore open.

"............"

The Manticore watched in silence.

At last, the girl's body crumbled inwards, like a mud sculpture left in the sun.

A purple smoke rose into the air.

The Manticore sucked the smoke into its mouth.

The smoke rose and rose, but the Manticore never stopped breathing it in, like a fish tank with the plug removed, sucking it all away. Its throat moved, swallowing it down.

When it had swallowed the last puff, the Manticore ran its tongue over its beautiful, lipstick red lips.

A drop of liquid slipped from the corner of its mouth and rolled off its chin. This drop of liquefied smoke was the color of blood and flesh.

There was no other trace of the girl, or of the smoke.

Oh ho ho!

Oh ho ho!

Oh ho ho ho ho ho…!

In the darkness, the Manticore laughed.

Her name was ancient Persian, and it meant 'Man-Eater.'

That delicate laugh bloomed like a morning rose, triumphantly extolling its evil.

Chapter Two
The Return of the Fire Witch

Suema Kazuko
second year, class D

1.

Recently, a strange rumor, or rather, a bit of a ghost story, has been spreading among the girls of the second year classes.

It's something about the mysterious Boogiepop.

Boogiepop is short, wears a black cape, and has a tall hat that's sort of like the one Maetel wore in *Galaxy Express 999*, only narrower. He's an assassin, and he can kill people instantly, without pain. He always does so when you are at your most beautiful, before you start to wither away, before you grow old and ugly.

Nobody knows where he's from, but most people seem to agree that he has something to do with the string of missing high school girls in the area.

Everyone wants to believe that the runaways were killed by an assassin that wanders in the shadows, fleeting as the morning mist…instead of running off to Tokyo or some other grim reality.

Reality is always rather dreary. When people vanish from it, it's natural to want to connect them to some sort of fantasy, to some other world.

"Hey, Suema, what was the actual case that inspired *The Village of Eight Graves*?" asked the girl in front of me, Kinoshita Kyoko, looking up from her crossword puzzle. I was eating my lunch one day shortly after the end of summer vacation.

"The Tsuyama Thirty," I said, without a second's thought.

"Hunh, Tsuyama Thirty…hey, it fits. Thanks."

Everyone eating with us was staring at me. "How *did* you know that?"

"You are *obsessed*."

"Don't be stupid, everyone knows *that*."

"We don't! Nobody does!"

"There was a book on it out last month," I replied, in a knowing manner as if to brush them off.

"*We* didn't *read* it! Why would we?"

"You're a little scary, Kazuko."

Everyone cackled.

"What kind of person can murder someone?" Kyoko asked, suddenly looking up from her crossword again.

"What kind? All kinds."

"I mean, like, who in this class seems likely to?" she said, lowering her voice.

"Oooh, do tell, do tell!" Everyone leaned closer.

"Uhhh, someone a little stiff, like they're off in their own little world and are kinda stubborn when it comes to stuff?" Even as I said it, I knew I might as well be saying her name.

"So…Kirima Nagi?" Yep, first name out; the most notorious student in our class. She was skipping today, apparently; no sign of her all morning.

"Hmm, well, she's not normal, that's for sure."

"Not normal? The Fire Witch is six kinds of crazy!"

"She's skipped two days since the new term started. Wonder if she'll even bother coming tomorrow…"

"She might as well not. Even when she does come, she causes trouble the moment she steps through the gates and gets herself sent right back home."

"Kya ha ha! Sounds like her!"

"So far as killing goes, I hear she actually *is*."

"How so?"

"You know, one slip and you miss your period…"

"Ah!"

"Then she gets herself suspended before anyone notices and takes care of it…"

"I believe it!"

There was no evidence at all, but that didn't stop them from talking.

Everyone was laughing, though, so I laughed with them.

I didn't hate her like they did.

Sure, she was trouble. But there was something about the way that she looked at people that was pretty cool; the way she didn't seem to care whether you were older or even a teacher, but just looked straight at you.

"She's got no parents, right?"

"Yeah, like, they live abroad or something? You heard she was the top scorer on the entrance exam, right? But she wasn't the speaker at the entrance ceremony. Know why?"

"Why?"

"Her guardian's name isn't Kirima."

"She's illegitimate?"

"Yeah. She just gets money and lives by herself in some apartment."

"No way…"

"So, she can do whatever she wants. Bring a different guy home every day, or like Suema says, 'Start killing.' She could have a mountain of bodies at her place, and no one would ever know."

"In the freezer?"

"All frozen up."

"Thaws them out and cooks them!"

"Ew, gross!"

Everyone laughed again.

I went along with them.

We laughed a bit too loud and Yurihara-san, who was sitting nearby, looked up from her study guide and glared at us. She was the best student in the class…and in the running for top of the school. I'd heard she'd taken practice tests at her cram school, and outscored students from the best schools in town three times running. She was also beautiful…and a little stuck up; meaning that she had no friends in our class. Even though she might've felt a little out of our league, she somehow knew that all it took was a cold glance to quiet us down.

"Maybe Nagi is Boogiepop?" Kyoko said.

"Ew, no. Boogiepop's a beautiful boy."

At the time, that was my first encounter with that name, so I felt myself compelled to ask about it.

"You don't know? But he's a killer!"

"It's not like I know everything."

They filled me in, but I'm into criminal psychology, and this was just some school horror story. God, it was beyond absurd. They made it out to be less of a serial killer and more like some crazed monster.

"Hmm…that's kinda scary." Everyone was watching, so I had to pretend to be alarmed.

"Kind of a turn-on, huh? Wonder how he kills them?" With that, they all started babbling away, swooning over this fantasy man of theirs.

Did he strangle them? Run them through with a knife? They kept suggesting rather time-consuming methods of killing, and I started to get irritated.

"Can we get your expert opinion?" Kyoko asked teasingly, suddenly turning to me.

"Sure…poison gas."

"Ew, like Sarin?" They all said at once.

"Nah, hydrocyanic acid gas. It's colorless and invisible, but very poisonous, and it kills you instantly. You can spray it on someone, and it vanishes quickly, leaving no evidence. The body isn't even dirty. Smells like peaches."

"Hunh…?" Everyone was staring at me, slightly creeped out.

'Oops,' I thought.

I'd done it again. I knew full well this kind of knowledge wouldn't interest them.

At this point, the class lady killer, Kimura-kun, came over and said, "What's up?" Everyone replied, "Nothing…" Apparently the Boogiepop stories were being kept secret from the boys.

A myth only the girls knew. It seemed I was the last one in class to hear about it.

I always am.

"………"

That depressed me a little, so I only half listened to their conversation, nodding when it seemed appropriate.

My interest in criminal and abnormal psychology stems from a personal experience I had.

Five years ago, in seventh grade, I was almost killed.

There was a serial killer hiding in our town, and he killed himself just when the police were about to catch him.

The killer took sexual pleasure in killing, which is freaky enough, but among the notes that he left behind was one with my address and a detailed account of the route that I took to school.

Had he not killed himself, it turns out that I would've been his next victim.

The police investigated my family to see if they had any connection to the killer, just to be certain. Of course, we'd never even seen him before. My parents tried to keep it a secret from me, but I found out when the police started questioning me directly.

I would be lying if I said it wasn't a shock.

But more powerful than the shock was the unreal feeling that it gave me.

My life had been in the hands of someone with no connection to me at all. I just couldn't wrap my head around the idea, which is exactly how I got interested in that sort of thing to begin with.

I never told my friends why.

I knew they would look at me differently if I did. "The psycho liked her," they would say, which is more than a good enough reason to put me on the bullied list. It was a bit too harsh of a truth to laugh off.

But just being interested in that sort of thing was enough to make me different, and the class tends to treat me like Doctor Murder, but it's a far cry from being bullied.

***

After lunch, we all went off to our fifth period classrooms.

Even though I was in the science program, my next class was Modern Japanese, a subject that automatically got on my nerves. Our school let you choose between science and humanities concentrations in your second year, but even so, we had to complete one course from the other program during our second year. An absurd requirement, if you ask me.

A friend from another class who was also forced to take Japanese walked across the covered walkway with me. Usually, there were three of us, but Niitoki-san was at a meeting for the discipline committee today.

As we walked, the PA came on that said, "…Miyashita Touka, second year, class C. Please, return to the infirmary at once. Miyashita Touka, second year, class C…"

"Hunh, wonder where Touka went?" the girl next to me asked. She was in the same class.

"She was in the infirmary?"

"Yeah, she got sick at the start of fourth bell…"

"Faking it?"

"Mm…she *is* dating a senior…"

"Skipping out for a date?"

"Maybe. But dating *is* against the rules, so don't tell Niitoki-san," she said, putting her finger in front of her lips.

I grimaced back at her. "I would never."

"They're probably on the roof or something now…" she said, glancing out the window. Suddenly, she let out a piercing shriek.

Startled, I asked, "Wh-what?"

"Th-th-th-there!" She pointed out the window, her finger trembling.

"What?"

"Boogiepop! On the roof!"

"Eh?" I stuck my head out the window.

But there was nothing.

"Nothing there."

"There was! I saw it! It moved away!"

"You sure it wasn't somebody else? Miyashita-san?"

"I don't think so! It had a black hat on! Like a pipe!" she said, still in a panic.

Clearly, she was seeing things, but nobody believes that when it happens to them. Reverse psychology was more effective. If I pretended to believe her, she would start listening to me.

"Okay. Let's go see," I said, and she spun to stare at me in horror.

"Hunh?"

"If Boogiepop is real, then I want to see him."

"No! Don't! It's dangerous!"

"Don't worry. Go ahead, I'll meet you in class."

I headed for the roof.

I ran up almost all of the stairs, and I was pretty out of breath by the time that I reached the door.

But the door to the roof was locked. Oh, right; they had belatedly sealed it off after someone had thrown themselves off.

I peered out the window. I could see most of the roof, but there was nobody there.

When I got down the stairs, she was waiting for me, looking worried.

"Wha-what happened?"

"Nothing there."

"Really?"

"Yep. I looked everywhere."

"Hunh. I guess I must have imagined it…" she said, relieved.

"I guess," I replied, surprised to find myself disappointed. As we headed to class, it occurred to me that there was a fire escape at the back of the roof, and if someone had gone down that, I wouldn't have been able to see them. But it was too late to go check now.

Nothing like that happened again, and our peaceful, safe lives dragged on.

2.

"Say, Suema, what are murderers thinking?" Kyoko suddenly asked me, one day late in fall, as we were on our way home from school.

"Eh, why?"

The two of us were walking along the bank of the river. Kyoko and I were the only two members of our circle of friends that walked to school, so we always went home together. Most students take the bus to school. Hardly anyone walks, so there was no one but us on the street.

"Oh, no reason," Kyoko dried up.

"You're always asking me stuff like that recently. What's up?"

"Oh, nothing. Never mind."

But there had to be a reason for it.

"Tell me."

"You see…" Kyoko whispered very quietly.

"Yeah?"

"She's suspended now, right?"

"Hunh? Oh, you mean Kirima-san?"

Two weeks ago, she'd been suspended for smoking on school grounds. She was due back the next day, though.

"Do you think…she would really kill someone?"

"Hah?" I doubted my own ears. Sure, she was the odd girl out, but Nagi was still our classmate. She hardly deserved to be called a murderer.

"What are you talking about?"

"You said it yourself…when was it? We were eating lunch…"

That had been a long time ago. I had completely forgotten.

"Uh, did I? I might have…"

"Do you really think so?" Kyoko was creepily serious.

"Even if I did say that, it was just an example," I hastily explained.

Kyoko's expression didn't change. "The girl is *scary*."

"Well, I'll grant that she's not easy to get to know…"

"She did something to this girl I know. She hasn't been the same since," her voice trembled. She meant it. She wasn't kidding.

"Something? What?"

"Threatened her, I think."

"For money?"

Kyoko shook her head. "No, not money. She's rich, you know."

"Yeah. She has her own apartment. Then what?"

Kyoko didn't answer.

Like anyone on earth would, I told her that I could keep a secret, but she still didn't say anything, so I asked, "Does it have anything to do with why Kirima got suspended?"

"I don't know…"

"You don't know?"

"I feel like she got herself suspended *because of* it…"
Kyoko said, but I didn't follow.

Come to think of it, Nagi had not been suspended for
smoking, but for having a cigarette in her lips.

And the place where she'd been caught—the teacher's
restroom. It would have been extremely strange if she had *not*
been caught. A female teacher had found her, and Nagi had
glared at her so fiercely that the she fled and got a male
teacher, making quite a fuss.

She made no excuses. Or apologies.

She never did.

I had never once heard her say 'sorry' during all the times that
the teachers had yelled at her.

One time, a teacher scolded her for staring out the window,
and Nagi had curtly quipped, "You're boring." However, her
grades were too good for the teachers to take any drastic
measures.

Still, she skipped a lot.

We're not just talking leaving a bell early, either. No, she
would drop the whole day; never even come to school…for
three days running! Yet when she came back, she knew
everything that we had covered while she was gone, and she
could answer any question that the teachers threw at her.

Nobody knew what she did when she wasn't in school
and no one ever had the guts to ask.

She was enigmatic and more than a little scary, so
somewhere along the line her nickname became "The Fire Witch."
Word had it that this was because she knew some form of black
magic, like the "Karma Dance," which sounded plausible enough.

Even so, it was hard to imagine that she had intentionally

gotten herself suspended. Suspensions went on your permanent transcript.

"That's going a bit overboard," I told Kyoko, but she didn't answer.

She stared up into the air, muttering, "She's gonna kill me…"

This I could not ignore. "Why? What for?"

Suddenly, Kyoko's entire body shuddered once, then froze. "Eeeeee!"

I followed her line of sight.

There was a girl standing on the road a short distance from us. She had been sitting on the bank, and stood up when we approached.

She wore an old, worn leather jacket and thick leather pants. There were metallic guards on her knees and elbows, like what bikers wear. Her slightly wavy hair was bound in a bandanna, and beneath her eyebrows, her eyes were less glittering than gleaming. She glared at us…at Kyoko.

"I've been waiting for you, Kinoshita Kyoko," she said, in her distinctive manly voice.

It was the suspended Kirima Nagi, in the flesh.

"No! Ahhh!" Kyoko screamed.

She fled behind me, shoving me towards Nagi.

Reeling, I almost smacked right into Nagi as she ran towards us.

But Nagi slid by me without so much as a glance in my direction and took off after Kyoko.

"W-wait!" I yelled as I hurriedly gave chase, but Nagi was fast. Looking closely, she was wearing big black boots. I thought they were rubber at first, but I was wrong. These were steel-toed work boots, the kind that construction workers wear.

The kind that can't be crushed, even if several tons fall on them. Kick someone with these, and they might as well die.

This was clearly not a fashion statement. It was a level beyond biker wear or air sneakers.

The bag on her back was strapped to her body, and didn't budge as she ran. It was like…

(…like she was dressed for combat?!)

No normal high school girl would ever dress like that. Not even a gang member.

She looked more like a hitman.

"H-help me!" Kyoko yelled.

Nagi snarled back, "You call for help, and you'll have to talk to the cops!"

That shut Kyoko up. She stopped in her tracks.

That was enough for Nagi; she closed the distance between them, and tackled her mercilessly from behind. Both girls hit the ground, sliding down the river bank.

Wheezing, I caught up to them to find Nagi twisting Kyoko's arm behind her. It looked just like a hold from something I'd seen on TV, like judo or kung fu. Kyoko couldn't move a muscle. We clearly hadn't learned this sort of wrestling at school.

"Ow! Ow! Ow! Let go!"

"Want me to go ahead and break it? Even you'll take some time to heal then, eh, Manticore?!"

I have no idea what she meant by that.

"No, don't! I'll never do it again, I swear!" Kyoko shrieked.

"Stop that, Kirima-san!" I cried, jumping on her, but she kicked me away.

She spoke to Kyoko again, "It's not just me. Echoes is looking for you too! Keep pretending and you'll lose an arm! And then, you won't have any hope of winning!"

What on earth was she talking about?

"I swear! I swear to God I'll never do drugs again! Please don't! Please!" Kyoko sobbed. Drugs?

"I know you killed Kusatsu Akiko! Don't lie to me!" Nagi roared.

I thought my heart was gonna stop.

Kusatsu Akiko—?

That was the name of a first year girl who had gone missing.

"I didn't! I didn't! It wasn't me, I swear! She just gave me the drugs!"

There was an unpleasant popping sound from Kyoko's arm.

Kyoko's eyes rolled up in her head.

"...Damn, you're normal!" Nagi snarled and let go.

Kyoko rolled down the bank.

"Kyoko!" I shouted, racing over to her and putting my arms around her.

"Don't worry. I stopped before the joint was destroyed. It'll hurt for a few days and then be fine," Nagi said.

Kyoko was trembling.

"What's going on?!" I screamed.

"You should ask Kinoshita herself, Suema-san," Nagi replied, her voice completely serene.

Kyoko's teeth were chattering. She'd been scared half to death. Understandably; so had I.

"This is going too far!"

"But it's better than getting arrested, right, Kinoshita?" Nagi said. Kyoko stiffened. "I hope you learn from this. Next time, you'll know better than to do stupid shit just because your friends do it."

She turned to leave.

"Wait!" I yelled.

Nagi looked at me, and said, "Suema-san, maybe it's time to let go of what happened five years ago. Get too hung up on something like that and *it'll come back to haunt you.*"

Her gruff voice matched her boyish face perfectly. But that wasn't the problem.

"H-how did—?"

How did she know I'd nearly been murdered five years ago?!

"H-hold on a minute…" I tried to stop her, but the Fire Witch stalked away without another word.

3.

I had to swear to keep it a secret before Kyoko would tell me anything.

"We…we were at the same Junior High. We were all on the table tennis team. Even in Junior High, we hung out together. Kusatsu was one of us, but a year younger. She was team captain when we were third years, so we sort of stopped thinking of her that way.

"So, three months ago, Kusatsu called to say she had something good, and that everyone should hook up with her.

"It was a weird sort of drug.

"No, not uppers; I think it was something else. It was a sort of bluish, see-through liquid. You took a sniff of it, and it was like your head opened up, like you became transparent, like every corner of your body was washed clean.

"Glue? No…I don't know, but it didn't have that strong of a smell.

"Kusatsu didn't tell us much, but she said some pharmaceutical company had created it as a test product. Yeah, it was probably bullshit. But, hey, it was free, so we all tried it out...

"Right. She never charged us anything.

"She was never exactly a generous person, so I'm not sure why...

"And a little while later, people from our group started running away.

"No, I don't know where they went! They didn't tell anyone. They just, you know, vanished. Yeah, girls from other schools too.

"And then, Kusatsu vanished. By this point, the rest of us were starting to wonder if it had something to do with the drugs. We didn't know where she got it, but maybe it was something nobody was supposed to know about it and they were taking us out. Then suddenly one of us announced that she wasn't gonna have anything to do with us any more.

"This made us nervous. We had to know why.

"She said Kirima Nagi had threatened her. Somehow, she had found out about the drugs, and she had told her to never touch them again...

"Not just the one, though. She hit every girl...in order. I was the last one.

"Started two weeks ago, right after she was suspended. That's why I said she had intentionally gotten herself suspended—so she would have a good reason for not coming to school, and so that she could move freely.

"No! I'm never touching drugs again!

"Hunh? No way! Why would I know Kirima Nagi?! I've always avoided her up to now.

"Please, don't tell anyone, Suema! Keep it a secret! I probably should never have told you either. But I had to. I just had to!

Keeping quiet was just too frightening…it was crushing me…"

I held Kyoko, comforting her until she stopped crying. Then we killed some time in a booth at *First Kitchen*, so that her face could return to normal before I took her back home.

It was night by then, and as I walked through the darkened streets, I thought things over.

Her fragmented story suggested that she had only seen a small part of what was really going on. I couldn't guess much from what she'd told me, but it sounded like she hadn't been one of the ringleaders of this group of ex-table tennis team players. More like she did whatever the much less stable girls told her to; just a third wheel, hanging on to the cool kids.

She wasn't even a victim. She was just in the wrong place at the wrong time.

Nagi had said Kusatsu Akiko had been killed…

And she knew about my past.

But…how?

Who was she?

Should I tell the school…or the police?

(But I promised Kyoko…)

If word got out that Kyoko had done drugs, that would be it for her—she'd be finished. It wouldn't end at suspension, either; she'd be expelled as an example to the other students. I didn't want to do that to her.

It was very dark outside.

The streetlight above me had clearly not been changed in years, and it was flickering madly.

"…………"

I stopped walking.

I opened my bag under the unsteady light, and thanks to my bad habit of carrying far too much stuff around with me all of the time, I was able to get out the class directory. It listed not only phone numbers, but also addresses.

I looked up the address of the person three names before my own.

Somewhat surprisingly, Kirima Nagi, like me, lived close to school. I could walk there.

(Okay, let's do it!)

I snapped my bag closed and walked as fast as I could in that direction.

But why did I have to meet her?

Kyoko, who was actually part of it, was running away as fast as she could. That was the more natural reaction. Anyone normal would do the same.

I was clearly a third party, and I had nothing to do with anything.

But I didn't *like* that.

Five years ago, things had all happened without me knowing about them. I only found out when everything was finished. My own will played no part in the matter.

If there was danger, I wanted to see it.

That's why I had chased after Boogiepop, even though there was clearly no such thing. It was all the same to me. I didn't care what it was…I just wanted to confront something.

(No more blissful ignorance for me.)

Kirima Nagi might really be a witch. I hoped she was.

***

"…Uh?"

I was standing on the right street, but there were no apartment buildings, only houses.

I checked the address again and again, but I was clearly in the right place.

But I couldn't find any house with the name "Kirima" on the gate. Checking the directory again, I noticed that it had "Taniguchi" written in very small characters next to it. She must live there.

(…must be that guardian with the different name.)

There *was* a house with "Taniguchi" on the gate, and the numbers seemed to match.

It was a really normal-looking home, a ready-built house like any other. A little on the wealthy side, but normally so.

Unable to connect it with Nagi's bizarre appearance during our earlier encounter, I hesitated, debating for a long time before I pushed the buzzer.

When I finally did, it made a half-hearted, ultra normal ding-dong sound.

"Who is it?" the voice from the intercom said, surprising me. It wasn't Nagi's voice, but rather that of a boy.

"Um, is, uh…is Kirima-san…?" I stuttered, all flustered.

"You're Nagi's friend?" the voice said quite cheerfully.

A moment later, the door swung open. The cheery boy stood in the doorway. He was taller than either Nagi or me, but younger, probably in Junior High. And that smile…it was friendly and warm.

"Come on in. But Nagi's not home yet, I'm afraid."

"O-oh, um…"

"Come in and wait. She should be back soon."

He led me to the guest room.

The inside was normal too.

There was even a set of little dolls in the shape of the zodiac signs sitting on top of the cabinet.

"Here," the boy said, putting a cup of tea and a plate of cookies in front of me.

"Uh, thanks." It was really good. I know nothing about tea, but I'm pretty sure this was what they called good tea.

"Gosh, I don't think I've ever met a friend of Nagi's before," the boy said airily.

"Y-you are…?" I asked.

"Her brother," he replied. They looked *nothing* alike.

"Um, I'd heard Kirima-san lived alone, so…"

"Yeah, I got here about six months ago. I lived abroad with my parents until last spring, but I've got entrance tests for high school next year, so I thought that I ought to get used to Japan first."

"Your parents…"

Nagi had parents after all. But why was their name Taniguchi?

At this point, we heard a voice call out, "I'm home," from the entrance. It was Nagi.

"In here," her brother said as he stood up and went to meet her.

"You brought *another* girl home?" Nagi said.

Her brother laughed. "This one's yours. She's been waiting for you."

I nearly yelped when Nagi came in.

She had changed into her school uniform, like she'd just come home from school.

"Oh, it's you," Nagi said quietly as I stood there speechless. "Let's go upstairs."

Following her lead, we went upstairs to her bedroom.

The polar opposite of downstairs, her room was free of decoration; nothing but computers and books. One bed, two desks. One was for studying, apparently, since the surface was empty. The other desk was for her computer—or, should I say, computers. It was kind of hard to tell just how many she had. There were multiple boxy computer towers and an assortment of other machines attached to them. She had three different monitors, all lined up next to each other. At first, I assumed two of them might've been televisions, but the screen savers were a dead giveaway. Worse, the pile of machinery spilled out onto the floor, filling nearly half of the ten-mat room. It felt less like a girl's bedroom and more like some mad hacker's secret lair. Much to my surprise, there were no signs of any black magic books at all. All the books that lined Nagi's shelves were merely an assortment of reference books and difficult looking hardcover tomes. Still, Nagi's collection of computer software boxes looked to have her book collection beat.

Nagi pulled the chair out from the study desk, and offered it to me. "Sit."

"Okay," I said, and did.

"Surprised?" Nagi grinned.

"Hm?"

"By Masaki. Everyone thinks I live alone."

"Um, yeah. I didn't know you had a brother."

"He's not my brother. We're not related," Nagi replied, shaking her head. "He's my mom's second husband's son from a previous marriage. He's a good kid, but a bit too good at manipulating me. Gonna grow up to be a real Don Juan. Sad."

"So, that's why his name's...?"

"Right, my mom's husband's name. I kept the old one."

"Hmm…why?"

"'Cause I've got a father complex," Nagi replied. I couldn't tell if she was joking.

"Your father is…?"

"I thought you'd know. Kirima Seiichi. Wrote a lot of books."

"Ehhhh?!" I interrupted rather loudly. "You're kidding!"

"Nope."

"But…the writer, Kirima Seiichi?!"

Of course, I knew him. I'd learned most of what I knew about criminal psychology or depth psychology from his books. *The Scream Inside - Multiple Personality Disorder*, or *When a Man Kills a Man*, or *Where the Killer's Mind Changes*, or *A Nightmare of Boredom*, or *The Proliferation of "Dunno"*, or *VS Imaginator*, and so on. He'd written far more summaries, essays and commentaries than novels. In fact, I'd never read any of his actual novels, just his scientific writings. He called himself a modern day enlightenment thinker, which is kind of hokey, but he did write an incredible number of books.

"That's my dad. He's dead now, though."

"Yeah, I knew that…but really? No, I mean really, really?"

"Why would I lie?"

"I know…but still…"

"You didn't think I had a strange name?"

"Never occurred to me. Wonder why not?"

Even as I asked, I knew the answer. I had unconsciously convinced myself that Kirima Seiichi or any other writer was hardly likely to live near me. Perhaps I wanted the people that I admired so much to live in some higher realm of existence than I did.

"Basically, I'm living off of the inheritance. Can't really beat it, either. Pays for school."

"Really? But your mother…"

"She wasn't married to him anymore. I got everything. She tossed her half away on her own. She was already a Taniguchi, and she didn't want anything to do with Kirima. That took care of taxes, so I pay rent here."

Here I was, just some normal girl from a typical middle-class nuclear family, and I'm sitting here, listening to the Fire Witch herself talking about her atypical life! Her whole situation just felt sort of unreal to me. It's no wonder that she acts the way she does. She'd hardly even been brought up in anything close to a proper environment.

Even so, there was something that I had to ask. "Um, so…"

"What? The reason?"

"Yeah. Why'd you save Kyoko?"

"My, my. You call that saving?" Nagi looked pleased.

"She told me everything. She got on some weird drug. You saved all of the girls from that, right?"

"Maybe I did…maybe I didn't."

"Why? How'd you find out? What did you do about it?" I was relentless.

Nagi simply stared back at me.

I felt my heart beating. She was certainly pretty. I felt like she might actually say, "I used magic."

What she actually said was, "My father died when I was ten."

"R-right," I stuttered, feeling like I should make some response. She carried on as if she didn't care if I was listening or not.

"My mother had already left us when he died, so there were only the two of us in the house. He never drank and he never chased after women. All he did was work. One day, I came home from school and found him lying on the floor. I called an ambulance, but all I could do was wait next to him as he spit up blood.

"He asked me, 'Nagi, what do you think about being normal?'

"I didn't know what he meant, so I shook my head.

"He said, 'Normal means you leave everything as it is and nothing ever changes. If you don't like that, you've got to do things that *aren't* normal. That's why I—'

"Those were his last words. He passed out and never woke up again. The cause of death was gastric perforation leading to dissolution of the internal organs. Disgusting way to die. I even heard that when the doctor cut his stomach open during the surgery, the smell was so bad that veteran nurses just started puking all over the floor.

"So what? I don't know. I just kind of gave up living normal after that."

She stopped.

When I said nothing in response, she added, "It's a messiah complex."

"R-really?"

From her face alone, you would think her a demure beauty. I found myself staring at her kind of thin lips, somehow unable to meet her eyes.

"I'm a psycho, all right. Got all the childhood trauma

anyone could want, right here."

She said disturbing things so easily.

But she didn't look like a monomaniac to me.

"But that's—" I started to say, but Nagi turned towards the computer behind her, cutting me off. She logged into one of the computers, loaded up some program, and hit a few keys.

A list popped up on one screen. It rolled upwards from the bottom of the screen. It appeared to be a list of people's names with numbers after them.

"Here," she said, pointing at the screen.

It read: *2-D-33 Suema Kazuko 8:25 AM-3:40 PM*

"That's…" I said, realizing that it was my very own attendance record.

"I'm logged into the school's network. You can get a basic outline of a student's movements with this. I noticed Kinoshita's group was suddenly getting worse, so I checked it out. Hit the drug story."

I was horrified. "Isn't this illegal?"

"Course it is," she said readily.

My mouth moved, but nothing came out.

"I have to," she said quietly. "Schools are kind of isolated from the rest of society. It's a strange environment where the police can't do jack. Something violent happens, whether it's caused by a student or a teacher, and the first thing that they do is try to cover it up. Even if someone dies, they'll take a cue from the times, and claim that it was a suicide caused by bullying, find some students who look like bullies, and just expel them for it…and that may well end up being enough, half the time."

"T-true, but…"

"I know it's wrong, but someone's got to do it. We sure as hell can't expect the teachers to."

"That's not what I mean, but…"

But who was this girl, who would intentionally get herself suspended to do any of this?

A messiah complex—

That was a creepy type of megalomania, in which you believed yourself to be some sort of savior.

In Kirima Seiichi's books, there was a case where a middle-aged man believed himself to be Batman, put on a costume and attacked an acquitted murder suspect. He wound up being killed himself, and the killer walked a second time, pleading self-defense. If the suspect had truly been innocent, the whole thing was a tragedy based on absurd principles, but if he had been guilty, then it was a tragedy in which justice had been utterly defeated by evil. Either way, it was a sad tale to recount.

This is how Kirima Nagi saw herself.

Certainly, Kirima Seiichi spent most of his time analyzing sinister phenomenon in the underbelly of the human mind, putting out books and articles on the distortions of reality that made people commit crimes, so if you wanted to, you could certainly make a case for him having a messiah complex as well.

That his daughter, particularly one who diagnosed herself as having a father complex, was the same, was not particularly odd, but—

When I sat there in silence, Kirima thrust a phone at me. Not one on the house's line, but undoubtedly one taken out in her name and paid for out of her own pocket.

"Call."

"Er…who?" My eyes widened.

Much to my surprise, Nagi replied, "Your house, of course. Tell them you're bringing a friend home for dinner, and that they should make extra."

4.

The next day, Nagi came to school, off her suspension. Kyoko avoided her, and despite chasing us down the day before, Nagi acted as if she didn't even know us. Right from the start of first period, she was slumped over her desk, sleeping soundly. The teachers said nothing, apparently letting sleeping dogs lie.

Nagi stood up to go to the bathroom once during break, and I slid out after her without letting Kyoko see me.

"Um, Kirima-san," I said.

"Mm?" She looked back remotely, clearly still half asleep. "Oh, you again. Sorry, but I'm gonna be up all night tonight, so I need to get some sleep while I still can. Talk to you later, okay?" Her business finished, she returned to class and went straight back to sleep.

"……"

I was itching to talk with her more about yesterday, but any attempts that I tried to make were clearly going to be thwarted.

I had ended up taking Nagi home for dinner the night

before.

Why? Because she said, "Your folks are probably excessively worried when their daughter comes home late, with what happened before and all. Tell them that you met me, and that you invited me over, since my parents are off on holiday."

Since she was right, I did as I was told.

Her non-blood relative brother said, "Come again," as we left the Taniguchi house. It was pitch black, the sun having long since set.

We set off on foot, with Nagi silently following after me.

Unable to stand the silence, I asked a foolish question. "Don't you ever show your soft side, Kirima-san?"

"Sure. I'm careful not to be too hardcore. When I want, I can play a normal girl." Her voice went up an octave as she said this, and she forced the corners of her mouth upwards into a dubious looking smile. Since she was a pretty girl, so it wasn't all that unnatural looking.

"Well, good," I said, laughing. It wasn't what I really wanted to ask her.

As I squirmed, she asked, "You're smart, aren't you?"

"I suppose…" I wasn't sure how to take this, coming from the girl who was the top scorer on the entrance exams and the top student in the school, as far as make-up test were concerned.

"I think so. That's why I explained to you what I did, you know?"

"Yeah. I won't tell anyone." I meant it. After all, no one would believe me.

She shook her head. "That's not what I mean. About Kirima Seiichi."

"Hm? What about him?"

"You've been studying from his books, yet his daughter is

doing this kind of stupid shit all the time. In other words, get out while you still can." Her shoulders slumped.

I stopped in my tracks and just looked at her. "Why do you say things like that?"

"Why? That mess five years ago has nothing to do with you. Let go of it. It'll come back to haunt you. It'll warp your personality…just like it has mine!"

"Why?"

"Why…" Nagi looked slightly irritated. "Do you want to end up like me?"

Her eyes glared at me, her face that of the Fire Witch. But I didn't pull back. I wasn't afraid any more. I glared right back into those eyes.

"How did you know that I was almost killed five years ago? I never told anyone."

Nagi stiffened. She'd made a mistake. "Um, I…that is…"

"You've barely spoken to anyone in class, so you must have assumed that Doctor Murder's past was public knowledge. But nobody knows. Just the people who were a part of it. Just my parents and the police."

Nagi turned her head to the side to avert her gaze.

"Oh my god."

Nagi remained silent.

"So it was you. You saved me."

They told us the killer hung himself. But that explanation had never sat all that well with me.

She had taken him out. Just like she had saved Kyoko.

"It…it's not important. It was a long time ago," she said, sullen.

"It's pretty dang important to me! I've been over this hundreds of times. Why am I still alive? I'm only alive because the killer went and killed himself? Yeah, that makes me feel real good, knowing that. That means that the only way that good things happen is if you just sit and wait for bad things to self-destruct. What kind of explanation is that?! It sucks! And you know what else sucks? That there's nothing we can do to make the world a better place."

Yes.

That was it.

Justice might well prevail in the end, but ordinary people like me had no guarantee of surviving that long. We might get killed on the whim of some serial killer first.

But even then, if we at least knew that there were some people fighting for us, it'd make things a lot easier to bear. If we knew these people had saved us, we'd feel much more alive than if we only survived because the bad guy just up and killed himself.

"That wasn't me," Nagi said coldly.

"Liar."

"That was Boogiepop. Ultimately."

Suddenly presented with the name of a fictional character, an urban legend, I was put off my stride. "Hunh?" I said, dazed.

"Never mind. The point is, you have nothing to feel responsible for," she said roughly. Her tone seemed to imply that she had been joking a moment before, evading my question.

"But I…"

"Please, I don't want to talk about it," she said, and bit her lower lip.

And so we walked on, without my having said the most crucial thing.

***

As third period began, Nagi was still asleep.

I found myself staring vacantly at the curve of her back.

She looked so isolated, so lonely.

I imagined saying so much to her. Stuff like, 'Kirima-san, all I wanted to do was thank you. Thank you for saving me. If you can't repay the person who saved your life, then there's something wrong with the world. Right?'

Sadly, I couldn't imagine how she would respond.

Her body twisted on her desk. As she did this, she moaned aloud.

The teacher finally lost it and shouted, "Kirima!"

Nagi's head rose slowly from her desk. "Wha?"

"What did I just say? On second thought, prove this formula!" The teacher slapped the blackboard behind me. His handwriting wasn't legible at the best of times, and having it rubbed away in places didn't help matters. All this made it next to impossible to read the whole equation if you hadn't taken notes during his lecture.

Nagi narrowed her eyes, staring at the board for a moment. "$a<b$, $ab>c$. When c is a rational number, $x=24$, $y=17/3$, $z=7$," she answered, and flopped back on her desk.

The teacher's face turned beet red. She was right.

We all giggled, but Nagi ignored us and went right back to sleep.

It was just another typical school day.

Her oddball behavior might be her way of preparing for her next fight, but to the casual onlooker, she just seemed insolent.

She stirred in her sleep again, moaning. The moan sounded oddly girlish, and I stifled a laugh.

After all, the Fire Witch had finished her suspension, and was back among us.

Interlude

Echoes wandered the town. The clothes he'd procured a week before were now mere rags, and the police had nearly arrested him as a suspicious character, when all he'd really done was just walk down the street. He'd been saved by some mysterious boy in a black hat, and managed to escape without hurting a soul. On the way here from the mountains, he had already been forced to seriously injure six people.

He knew the Manticore was near.

But human towns were built too close together, and the people living in them all seemed to congregate together. He had no idea how to find the Manticore here.

"…………"

As the sky grew darker, he found himself in a back alley, and once more, he collapsed on the ground.

This time, there were no people around. The alley smelled of rancid water.

"…………"

He looked up at the evening sky, but he couldn't see the stars here. In the mountains, he had been able to see them even in broad daylight.

But he couldn't cry any longer. The boy in the black hat had told him, "You're chasing something. Cry when you have found it."

This was true.

He could not rest here.

He had to stop the Manticore's slaughter. The Manticore was made from him. It was his child.

She had the power of communication that even he lacked, not to mention the powers that let him blend in with this planet's ecological system. This "transformation power" in particular could do untold damage to the environmental balance of this planet's primarily human civilization and prevent him from carrying out his main objective.

His objective—

He had to fulfill it. That was why he had been created. But the Manticore's existence was a hindrance to his objective, to his decision.

He had to make a decision, one way or the other.

That decision had to be rigorously balanced. Like him, the Manticore was alien to this planet and should not exist here. He had to dispose of her.

"…………"

He staggered to his feet.

There was a scream. A young women had come into the alley and caught sight of him.

He waved his hands trying to show that he meant no harm. But he didn't need to.

"What are you doing here?" the woman asked, coming towards him. It had not been a scream of terror, but simply surprise. "Oh no, you're hurt! How did this happen?"

On closer inspection, the woman was still a girl.

Without any reluctance, she wiped the blood from the wound on his head with an expensive looking designer handkerchief. The wound itself had long since healed, and he felt no pain from it, but the blood was still there, dried to his skin.

"H-hurt…" he said, trying to explain that it did not need tending. But there were few words in her speech for him to *return* and he could not produce a phrase with meaning.

"What should I do? Call the police?"

"P-police…" was all he could say.

But somehow the girl understood what he meant from this.

"No police, hunh? Okay. Where's your house? Nearby?"

He picked some words from her speech, forcing a sentence. "No—hou-house." When he spoke to people, he could only return words they had spoken, so as to not provide them with information beyond the limits of their under-standing.

"Homeless? Looks like you're in some kind of trouble."

He nodded. He waved his hands, telling her to back away from him.

She patted him gently on the shoulder. Body language for "calm down."

"No way, José. I leave you here and I won't be able to sleep at night."

Somehow, she seemed to understand what he wanted to say, even though he could not speak directly.

"Hmm, let me see…for the moment, let's put you in school. There's a card reader at the gate to get in, but I think I know a back way in."

"Sch-school…"

"Yeah, I live in an apartment building, but there are prying eyes everywhere. See? You aren't the only one with problems," she said jokingly, and grabbed his arm, pulling him forcibly to his feet. Then she dragged him after her.

He didn't know what else to do, so he followed her.

'Who was she?' he thought, and almost instantly she answered, "Me? My name's Kamikishiro. Kamikishiro Naoko. I'm a senior at Shinyo Academy. You?"

"Ah...oooh..." he couldn't answer. He was not allowed to provide humans with information about himself.

"You can't talk?"

"Can't...ta-talk."

"You're talking now. Hmm...they call you *Echoes*? Strange name. Almost like it was made for me to call you by."

Kamikishiro giggled. She had not yet noticed that she was understanding things that he had not said.

She smiled at him. "Don't worry. I know this kooky girl named Nagi. Anytime there's trouble, we talk to her and she usually takes care of it. Assuming you aren't a bad guy, Echoes," she finished with a wink.

She pulled out a cell phone, thumb flying over the keys, dialing this Nagi person with a practiced motion.

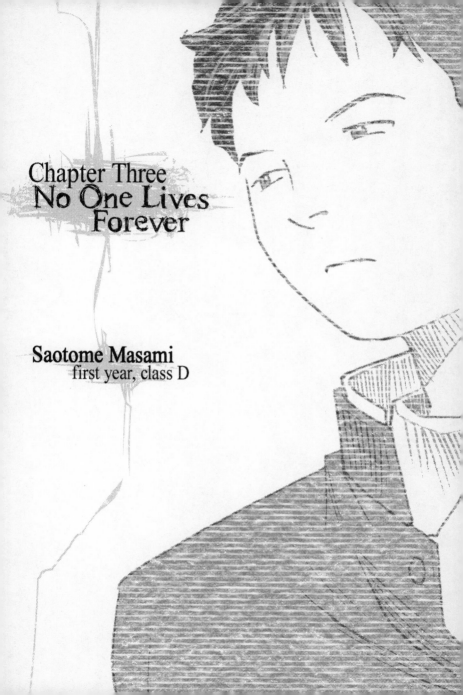

Chapter Three
No One Lives Forever

Saotome Masami
first year, class D

1.

First year student Saotome Masami first fell in love when he was fifteen. Until that point, he had never opened his heart to anyone and simply remained a 'nice guy' to the people around him. Needless to say, this was a major turning point in his life.

***

"Saotome-kun, you free Sunday?" asked his classmate Kusatsu Akiko, shortly after the start of the second term as they were performing their after-school cleaning duties.

"No plans to speak of."

"See, Sachiko has some free movie tickets, and she said we should all go together." Akiko had dark skin and high cheekbones. She looked at Masami, waiting for an answer.

"We?" Masami asked, leaning on his broom. This lowered his face to her line of sight. He was tall, with a face that had just enough charm to get him compared to pop idols. But it was always a different person every time, never fixing on one resemblance.

"You know Sakamoto-kun from class F? He made a pass at Sachiko and got the tickets, but she's a little nervous about going it alone."

"So, you need a discipline committee member as an escort? I know Sakamoto pretty well, and I don't want to drag his feet."

"Oh, you don't need to...well, maybe you do," Kusatsu Akiko said, smiling weakly at him. She was pretty forthright with everyone else but Masami, but she couldn't contradict him directly, because she was in love. Masami was well aware of this, and privately, he was annoyed by it. Until now.

But today, he simply smiled back at her instead.

"But if you just want me to tag along, fine. Not like I've got anything better to do. If we run into the guidance teacher on patrol, I can probably talk us out of trouble."

Kusatsu Akiko's face brightened. "Really? Well, the truth is, Sachiko's secretly pleased that Sakamoto-kun asked her, so I don't think you'll need to intervene."

"Whatever."

They both laughed.

You could never call Kusatsu Akiko a good-looking girl, but when she smiled next to the far more evenly-featured Masami, she gleamed like a still image from a soap opera.

***

When the four of them met at the station, they appeared to be a very close-knit group. They ran into Masami's *sempai* on the discipline committee, Takeda Keiji, and he took one look at them and asked if they were "double dating." So, there was clearly a hint of romance in the air.

The movie was a big Hollywood action movie, part three in a series, neither harming anyone nor doing anyone any good. The only part that Masami enjoyed was a bit where a minor villain was shot in the chest and knocked over backwards. His arms were flung out to the sides, and he slid backwards like a figure skater. In Masami's eyes, he looked light and free.

They left the theater, and a passing group of teenagers glared at them murderously. Walking quickly, faces grim, they all carried bags with large square lumps inside.

"Cram school?" asked Noguchi Sachiko, this evening's instigator. "I hope we never end up like that."

"Yeah," Kusatsu Akiko nodded. Masami remembered her letting it slip that she couldn't go to college, because her father's company was about to go bankrupt.

"That's a long time from now. We ought to enjoy ourselves while we can," Sakamoto Jun said, trying to distract Noguchi Sachiko.

"Yeah, just forget about it. Just live your life. Not like you can live forever," Masami said breezily.

"Oh look, it's Yurihara from our school," Noguchi Sachiko said, pointing.

Yurihara Minako, second year, class D, one of the best students in the school, and legend had it that she consistently beat out the best students at other cram schools on their practice tests. But she didn't look at all like the brainy type. Heck, she didn't even wear glasses. Instead, she had long straight hair with the kind of shine that no amount of treatment could ever give. It matched her slender face, giving the impression of a Heian era princess.

Yurihara Minako passed by them as they whispered, walking at a slower pace than the other students, and vanished into the cram school.

"She's so relaxed. You can just see the aura of her genius."

"You know she was scouted by some prep schools, right?" Sakamoto said with a knowledgeable expression.

"Really? They can do that?"

From the fuss that they made, you would never have thought that they were talking about a *sempai*.

All the while, Masami remained quiet, smiling to himself. He didn't even glance at Yurihara Minako.

They had promised not to let their eyes meet in public.

"Anyone up for karaoke? There's a place near here with a great track list," Kusatsu Akiko said brightly. She was in a good mood, now that she was out with her beloved Masami.

In the karaoke box, Masami sang easy pop songs, ones that had been all the rage up until recently, but had passed their peak, and everyone was starting to get sick of them now. He almost always sang that sort of song at karaoke. He preferred an American band called The Doors, which had broken up ages ago (long before he was even born) when the lead singer died of a drug overdose. But he never told anybody. The Doors weren't in a lot of karaoke machines, but he never sang them even if they were.

He had a good voice, but since everyone was a little tired of his selections, they never really seemed all that interested.

He always applauded other people's performances, never forgetting to keep up appearances. He never stuck out, was occasionally a little scorned, but he never made anyone jealous, and no one ever realized that he was keeping them at a distance.

He bought drinks for everybody. He took them directly from the tray when the waiter brought them and even passed them around himself.

He put Kusatsu Akiko's drink in her hands. Nobody saw him drop a small tablet, about five millimeters across, into her cup before he handed it over. Yurihara Minako had 'synthesized' the tablet, and as promised, it quickly dissolved into the diet cola. Kusatsu Akiko never noticed a thing.

2.

The first girl that Saotome Masami fell in love with was a second year student, Kirima Nagi. He told her this in May. She rejected him quite harshly.

"Sorry, but I don't have the time," was all she said.

"Is...is it because I'm younger?"

"No, not really...you're normal, right? Me? I'm nothing but trouble. Thanks, but sorry."

"O-okay." He was far less hurt by this than he'd expected. Quite the opposite; he found himself rather relieved to be brushed off coldly.

It was two months before he identified the source of those feelings.

***

"Hey, Saotome, you take Kusatsu home. I'll take care of Noguchi," Sakamoto whispered in Masami's ear as their time in the karaoke box ran low.

"Sure. Good luck," Masami whispered back.

As the four of them left the shop, Kusatsu Akiko suddenly proclaimed, "I...I don't feel so good." Her face was white as a sheet.

"That's too bad. I'd better take you home," Masami said, putting his arm around her shoulders.

"Uh, hang on! Saotome-kun!" Noguchi Sachiko cried, all flustered. She was about to be left alone with Sakamoto.

"You two have fun. Don't worry, I'll look after her."

"Er, but..."

"You heard the man. Let him go," Sakamoto said, cajoling. As the men had planned, they split off into two pairs. Noguchi Sachiko was steamrolled under Sakamoto's promises that he wouldn't "try anything."

Afterwards, he did get her to a hotel, where they had relations, but Noguchi Sachiko's parents found out and her old-fashioned father stormed the school, tracked Sakamoto down, and cursed him out in front of everyone. But in all the fuss, the two of them never had a moment to notice the events that followed. They had completely forgotten they were ever with Saotome Masami that night.

"Bye!"

"Yeah," Masami replied, as the four became two.

"I feel sick..." Kusatsu Akiko's voice grew gradually weaker in Masami's arms.

Masami never spoke a word. He simply hauled her along as if she were a piece of luggage. The silence was deafening.

Kusatsu Akiko was in no condition to be insulted. Her face was well beyond pale; you could see the blood vessels under her skin.

Not caring, Masami dragged her into the backroads. All they did was leave the lights and noise of the main drag for a narrow back road, but it was as silent as a graveyard, seemingly light years from the bustle of the city.

Before them was a giant parking garage that had failed in its bid to reopen and been abandoned. The land was intended to become an office building, but the owner had been unable to find any clients, and he had no other choice but to make it into a parking garage. As luck would have it, the owner had then gone bankrupt, and it was now just another of the country's forgotten bad debts.

Masami slipped between the railings of the surrounding fence, holding Akiko under his arm. She said nothing. She had already stopped breathing.

He dragged her up to the seventh floor of the parking lot. This far up, there was no chance of them being disturbed by thrill seekers.

Leaving Kusatsu Akiko on the ground, Masami stuck his face outside. It was pitch black all around them. Even if a normal human on the ground had been looking upwards, they could never have seen him.

He looked at his watch. It was a digital watch with a backlit screen. Unlike radial watches, it had the advantage of not making a sound.

The time confirmed, he nodded to himself.

Staring into the blackness below him, he waved his hands.

There was a small noise from far below him, like someone pushing a tack into a board.

Within an instant, a human shape appeared in the air in front of Masami.

It was a girl.

The shape slid past Masami, entering the parking lot. It landed right at the top of its arc, and there was no sound as its feet touched the floor.

The girl had jumped all the way to the seventh floor.

The girl turned towards Masami. She had long, bountiful, black hair plastered to her head. She had a cram school bag in her hand.

It was Yurihara Minako.

"Were you successful?" she asked.

Masami nodded. "Over there," he said, pointing to Kusatsu Akiko's corpse, which lay on its side, no longer moving.

"That one? The other girl was better," Yurihara said, frowning. Agitation could not be farther from her mind.

"Not really. This girl has friends all over. Lots of friends from Junior High," Masami replied, voice devoid of warmth.

"Does she? Then fine. You know more than I do, Saotome-kun." Yurihara handed her bag to Masami. He took it like an obedient little hotel bellboy whose only job is to serve.

Yurihara stooped down in front of Kusatsu Akiko.

"Mmm…seems like a waste not to eat her *now*," she said, her beautiful face contorting.

"Yeah, but if we use her, you'll be able to assimilate four or five more in no time," Masami chuckled. "For now, we wait, Manticore."

"Human society makes it hard to move." Yurihara the Manticore said, sighing. She lowered her face next to Kusatsu Akiko's.

Her long hair started to get in the way, so she held it back with her fingers, and kissed the corpse tenderly.

Her tongue pried the body's mouth open, forcing a gaseous form of the essence manufactured inside her body into Kusatsu Akiko.

Watching this monstrous, sinister spectacle unfolding in the darkness, Masami was entranced. As if he felt sexual pleasure, his face was even more ecstatic than at the moment of ejaculation.

For thirty long seconds, Yurihara kept her lips pressed to the corpse's.

Finally, she pulled away, wiping her mouth with the back of her hand. Her lips were bright red, but not from lipstick—the color did not rub off on her hands.

The color of her skin was so sleek she appeared to be wearing makeup, but this was also her natural state. When she had copied the real Yurihara Minako, she had copied the makeup as well.

"She should be revitalized momentarily," Yurihara said, with a satisfied smile.

"Hmm…" Masami said doubtfully. To make sure, he kicked the corpse lightly. Its fingers twitched. "Good."

Bit by bit, the entire body began shaking violently, as if it were lying on top of a high voltage electric fence.

Then the torso shot upwards, as if on a spring.

The eyes and mouth popped open, and a blue liquid, neither tears nor saliva, came pouring out of them.

"Woah! Can't let that touch me," Masami said, backing away from the sweet scent wafting off of the volatile liquid.

"Yes. For humans, it will work like a drug. It would not do for you to become addicted as well, Saotome-kun." Yurihara placed herself between Masami and Kusatsu Akiko. "Look here, woman," she ordered.

The no longer dead Kusatsu Akiko did as she was told, slowly rolling her head towards Yurihara. The flow of liquid had stopped.

"I have given you power. Power to corrupt humans. Use this power to supply me with more humans."

In normal society, Yurihara's words were unthinkable, but the previously dead girl nodded.

"Corrupt them well. When they suddenly vanish, we want the humans around them to assume that this was the logical next stage of their recent poor behavior. Including yourself."

Behind her, Masami nodded proudly, like a parent whose son had just correctly answered a question on visitor's day.

Yurihara whispered, "You have no memories of what happened here. You went bad of your own free will…"

3.

Five minutes later, Masami was walking along the street, once again supporting Kusatsu Akiko.

"Mm…mm?" Her fainting spell ended, and her eyes opened. "Wh-where are we?"

"Ah, good. You're awake," Masami said, stepping away from her.

"Eh? I was asleep? Oh no! Why didn't you wake me?" Kusatsu Akiko asked, quite flustered.

"I shook you several times."

"Oh no! I'm sorry! I wonder what…uhhh…" She tried to figure out the last thing she remembered, but she couldn't remember a thing. Obviously, it never occurred to her that she had died and was now merely functioning as a puppet, thanks to the stimulus of the drug.

"You're pretty heavy, you know that? It was hard work carrying you," Masami said sternly.

Kusatsu Akiko turned bright red, but for some reason, she wasn't that hurt by his words.

They parted ways in front of the station.

"See you at school tomorrow."

"Yeah…don't tell anyone about tonight. Especially…" she started to say a name, but trailed off.

She felt like there was a boy who she really didn't want to see her in an embarrassing moment like this, but for the life of her, she couldn't remember his name or what he looked like.

"Especially who?" Masami asked, with a knowing smile.

"Mm…never mind," Kusatsu Akiko's love had vanished with her memories.

"I had fun today," Masami said kindly.

But she simply replied, "Oh?" as if she didn't care at all, and turned her back.

She felt like there was a big, gaping hole in her heart, but she had no way of telling that her will and spirit were swiftly vanishing.

Masami paused to watch Kusatsu Akiko venture into the station, then swiftly turned on his heel and walked back into the city.

Yurihara was waiting at the Tristan coffee shop. She was seated in a booth towards the back.

"It went well?" she asked. She was wearing glasses and had her hair in a sauvage style. Masami knew that Yurihara could control her hair at will, but these quick hairstyle changes always took a moment to get used to.

"Yeah, her emotions are already fading," Masami replied. He sat down and ordered lemon tea and marron cake to soothe his sweet tooth. "Without knowing what she's doing, she'll make all of her friends try a drug that even she doesn't remember getting."

"Like a sleepwalker in the night, she'll regurgitate the fluid made by the cells in her body. She won't even try to figure out where it comes from. Her brain is shrinking, and she can't be bothered to make decisions on her own."

They looked at each other and giggled.

From the side, they looked like any peaceful, harmless young couple. But Saotome had already sacrificed the lives of three girls to Yurihara—the monstrous man-eater known as the Manticore.

They had met two months before, just before summer vacation.

Masami was a member of the tea ceremony club, largely because it never did anything. He had heard that it was a good idea to have been a member of a club in high school when it came time to apply for universities or jobs. Yurihara Minako was a member as well. Much like Masami, she hardly ever bothered to show up for the infrequent meetings that the club tended to have.

One day, it suddenly started to rain in the evening, despite blue skies all afternoon. The whims of summer. Masami had not planned to go to the club meeting, but since he had no umbrella, he thought he might as well kill some time in the tea room. He turned around at the shoe boxes at the entrance to school and went back inside.

The tea ceremony club didn't have a room of their own; they simply borrowed a room that was usually used for student guidance, as it was the only Japanese style room in the school. The faculty sponsor was the assistant principal, Komiya, and he was much too busy to ever show his face at meetings.

That day, the room was deathly silent and there was no

sign of any other students.

Next to the door was the tea ceremony club attendance book. If your name was written in this, it appeared that you had attended the meeting. Even if you rarely came, as long as your name showed up in the book, you were treated like an active member and could stay on the rosters.

Masami opened the book, and was about to write the date and his name, when he realized there was already an entry for that date. Someone else was here.

Yurihara Minako.

"……?"

Even if she had gone to the bathroom, it was strange that she hadn't left her bag. Before now, Masami had never even had the slightest interest in Yurihara Minako. She had a reputation for brains and beauty, but she never mattered to him in the slightest. And, like many a man before him, he had always been baffled by the idea of beauty.

He had already lost his virginity in Junior High to a girl with a face covered in zits and who was widely reputed as being rather ugly. Their relationship was kept secret, but less because he was embarrassed and more because he just didn't want to listen to everyone else's shocked commentaries on the subject. He didn't think anything at all about dating an ugly girl. In fact, after she started dating him, her pimples vanished and actually she became quite pretty. She soon left him for another boyfriend. But Masami wasn't particularly upset. He had never actually loved her to begin with; he simply used her to relieve his sexual appetites. Instead, she ended up crying and apologizing, even though it had been her idea to break up in the first place.

Masami no longer remembered her name and he couldn't remember Yurihara Minako's face all that clearly either. He knew she was supposed to be good looking and that she had good grades, but that was about it.

"Sempai, you there?" he asked, taking off his slippers and stepping onto the *tatami* in his socks.

He opened the *shoji* leading into the inner room. It was less of a room than a storage area for tables and cushions.

The moment he opened it, his eyebrows leapt upwards.

In the storage area, Yurihara Minako was upside-down against a pile of cushions, face twisted around so that it faced the same direction as her torso. Her head was on backwards. Her neck was broken with her spine clearly severed. Her eyes were open and empty.

She wasn't moving…at all.

She was dead.

The first thought that flashed through Masami's mind was relief that he had not written his name in the attendance book. He didn't want to get mixed up in something like this.

He took a step backwards.

This saved his life.

A hand with razor sharp claws passed through the air just in front of his face.

Some hidden killer had attacked him.

(*What*—?!)

He looked up.

There was a naked girl clinging to the ceiling, hands and feet thrust in the cracks between the wood paneling. He thought it was a woman, but only assumed this because he couldn't see any male genitalia between its legs. Later, he was to learn that there was no genitalia there at all.

The girl grinned. "You saw me," she whispered. "Now that you have seen me, I cannot allow you to live," she continued as if she were sharing a joke. If there had not already been a corpse lying beneath her, he would not have taken her seriously.

Masami was stunned. He simply stared blankly up at her, immobile.

If he had been a girl, he would have heard the legends. He would have thought, 'It's Boogiepop!'

She moved like the wind. She kicked Masami in the chest, sending him flying into the opposite wall before he knew what happened.

"—Gah!" He yelled as his back slammed into the wall. He moaned in pain, "Unh…" and was about to pass out, but he knew deep down that he couldn't let himself succumb to his body's frailties.

She laughed softly as she approached. There were traces of mud and leaves on her body. The mountains behind the school ran deep. She had probably ventured through them and come out at the school.

She looked like a majestic wild animal with a strange beauty about her; a strange fearlessness that he had never seen anywhere else, and an established aloofness found only in things that were beyond human understanding.

Masami simply stared up at her.

"Nice timing. I had just thought that it would be better to copy a male than a female. I shall take your shape," she said, reaching out towards Masami.

As if freed from possession, he blinked and said, "Wha-what?" He frowned, "C-copy?"

"Yes. I shall become you and blend into human society. No one will ever be able to find me."

"Hunh," his face scrunched up, but not because he felt despair at the sight of his approaching demise. No; the next thing he said was, "In that case, it would be far more effective to keep me alive." He sounded a little put out by this.

The girl frowned. "Why...?"

"Oh, you'll just have a much easier time as a stuck up teacher's pet with no friends at all like our little Yurihara Minako here. If you try to take my place, people will notice the difference. I've strived to maintain at least a mid-level of popularity here. People know me."

He sounded deeply disappointed by this. That's because he was.

He wanted to be killed by something much more powerful than him. Even with Kirima Nagi, he had not really wanted to date her; he had wanted her to kill him.

This was his nature. And for the first time, he understood this clearly.

He didn't know why exactly. There was obviously nothing out of the ordinary happening at home, and he had no childhood trauma to contend with, like Suema Kazuko had almost encountered. But there it was, clear as day.

If you searched really hard for a reason, it was a reaction against his life style—a way for him to fight against his deliberate pretense of mundanity. But this was far too shallow a reason to satisfy a psychiatrist. People like Masami, with a fetish for indirect suicide, were not particularly unusual.

"……?" The naked killer looked down at him, baffled. Until now, everyone who had ever seen her had felt nothing but hatred and fear, but this boy showed no signs of either. "Why are you so quiet? You do not struggle…you do not beg?" she found herself asking.

"That's because I love you," Masami answered, honestly and quite sincerely.

"Hunh?" For the first time in her life, the girl was dumbfounded.

***

"You were right, Saotome-kun. Yurihara Minako's form fits my needs well. Nobody thinks it strange if I don't talk to them in class. She was always like that, apparently," the Manticore said, in the dimly lit coffee shop. Her face so perfectly matched Yurihara's that for all intents and purposes she was Yurihara Minako, as the former owner of that name had long since been erased from the face of the earth.

"I thought so."

"The classes at school resemble some sort of game, but this studying for exams is utterly pointless. I just have to read the explanation and I can understand anything."

"You're much smarter than most of us humans then."

"Even Yurihara Minako's parents haven't noticed the difference. They communicate with her so cautiously. Are all humans like that?"

"Mostly. But be careful. There are a few egoists who think other people are a part of themselves. My parents, for example."

"Shall I kill them for you?" Yurihara suggested airily.

"Not yet. It's still too early," Masami replied just as evenly.

"True. We must be cautious until we control the world," she giggled.

"Exactly," Masami grinned back.

At this point, the waitress brought the lemon tea and cake that Masami had ordered. She overheard them talking about 'controlling the world,' but just assumed that they were talking about some sort of new video game.

But she did think that the couple was far too horny, though, and that they should get a room before they started making out right there in the restaurant.

'They can't even be out of high school yet, but they're acting like newlyweds. They're all over each other!" she thought. She was still reeling from a harsh break up, so she slapped the bill on the table a bit roughly and left.

Masami carried on, "Should we make ourselves any new slaves beyond Kusatsu Akiko?"

"Yes, if possible, I'd like two or three more. Too many, and we might get noticed, though…but at some point, we'll need them on a larger scale. Better to test the process out now."

Their plan was simple: remake human society with themselves at the center. Yurihara certainly had the power to make that a reality. She could become any human she wanted and could make any human do her bidding.

The idea was Masami's. He offered to cooperate with her, but when she told him of her powers, he found himself rubbing his hands together with glee.

"We can use that," he said eagerly.

When she heard his plan, it sounded quite reasonable, so

she agreed. All she'd thought about before now was her own survival. She'd never actually thought about the rest of the world. And more importantly, she had always been alone. She'd been cloned as an 'experiment' and had no family of her own. The only person who had ever told her "I love you" was Saotome Masami, whom normal society would classify as a crazed lunatic.

"But there must be agents from the 'institution' pursuing me. What should we do about them?"

"At the moment, all we can do is hope that they don't find you. Give it a little more time, and we'll be able to fight back."

"And demolish anyone who wishes to 'erase' me as a 'failure'?"

"Exactly! You're no failure. You're going to be the new ruler of the world," Masami said forcefully.

Yurihara rested her hand on top of his. "Saotome-kun, you are my prince." The man-eating monster stroked the hand of her Mephistopheles, while sweetly whispering, "I love you." It may have been twisted, but they were unmistakably in love.

4.

As they had planned, Kusatsu Akiko gradually began to come to school less and less often. Her family was falling apart, and was behind on her tuition payments, so nobody thought this at all unnatural.

She got her friends hooked, and Yurihara and Masami took them. The first one they nabbed was Suzumiya Takako, second year, class F.

It was easy to take her. She and her friends always gathered in seclusion, and all that Yurihara and Masami had to do was follow them as they left and simply take them down.

Unfortunately, they were unable to alter them in the way that they had Kusatsu Akiko. They died, but they did not return.

"It seems it requires a very delicate balance."

"Good thing we decided to experiment first," they said, whispering in the darkness.

They had been killing Shinyo Academy and other local high school girls, one after another. To cover this up, they laid down a few red herrings to throw off the authorities.

Once the precedent was established, the rest of their work went smoothly. There were no signs of fuss at school. At Shinyo Academy, there had even been a special meeting and a resulting morning lecture, but that was all. Missing person reports had probably been filed with the police, but they were buried in a mountain of missing girls totally unrelated to them at all, and swiftly forgotten about.

"The students that ran away were all slackers to begin with," the guidance teacher told Saotome at the discipline committee meeting.

This generalization was so insensitive to the students' individual circumstances that the committee president, Niitoki Kei, stiffened her tiny body and turned her cute, childish face downwards to hide her steaming glare.

But Masami was taking minutes, so he wrote the gist of the comment down in his notebook. "Disturbance in behavior precedes disappearance." As he wrote these words, he was expressionless.

He never let a faint smile steal across his lips.

Everything was going exactly according to plan.

Still, he was left expressionless. Nothing the teachers said and nothing happening around him could change this. He had killed five people without so much as remorse, and here he was, still acting like an ordinary student.

But when the teacher stated that, "Incidentally, the infamous Kirima Nagi failed to arrive this morning. Make sure to keep an eye on her, hear? No telling what that girl's plotting in the shadows," Masami's cold heart skipped a beat. He didn't show it, but even now that he had the Manticore, hers was one of the few names that could affect him.

***

Kusatsu Akiko's behavior became strange a month after she had been altered.

Even when she came to school, she seemed particularly out of it.

When people spoke to her, she barely seemed to notice, much less reply.

(...uh-oh.)

Masami figured that Kusatsu Akiko had begun to break down much faster than expected.

They couldn't leave her like this. She was clearly evidence. If she collapsed somewhere and was taken to a hospital, they would surely discover her condition, and the 'institution' that made the Manticore would soon find out.

So Yurihara was forced to eat Kusatsu Akiko, and the first stage of their experiment ended. Unfortunately, they had still not managed to recruit a second subject with any real success, and it was putting considerable strain on both Masami and Yurihara's relationship.

"Damn it! Why doesn't it work?!" Yurihara yelled, growing ever more high strung.

"It's nothing to worry about. We will have many more opportunities."

"I know that, but..." Yurihara said, and then looked up at Masami. "I'm sorry. I'll get it right next time."

"We should wait a while," Masami replied calmly.

"Why? I can do it now!" Yurihara said almost shrieking, her voice clearly echoing through the empty parking garage.

"That's not the problem. We're reaching the limit of what

we can do in the school. We have to look for more prey elsewhere. But we need to prepare. Not only for more experiments, but for your food supply as well. We've taken care of both of them at the same time so far, but you need other forms of nourishment, don't you?" he said gently, his tone showing a marked contrast to the horrific meaning behind his words. He rested his hand on her shoulder.

"All right, we shall do as you say." Yurihara nodded obediently.

***

The day after Kusatsu Akiko vanished, Masami got involved in something a little out of the ordinary.

During break, he was on his way back from returning a slide ruler he'd borrowed from the teacher's room, when a female teacher came flying around the corner, extremely flustered.

"Y-you! You're on the discipline committee, aren't you?!" she asked, her face brightening the moment she saw Masami.

"Yes, Saotome, 1-D," Masami replied.

"Thank god you're here! Please keep watch! Don't let her get away!" she shouted, and continued on down the hall.

"……?" Masami looked puzzled, and walked in the direction that she had come from. It was the staff bathroom.

Since it had been a female teacher, he poked his head through the door. He had no particular enthusiasm for ladies restrooms, but he didn't hesitate at all in his actions. He simply walked straight inside.

But once inside, he was badly shocked.

"Oh, it's you, Saotome-kun," said Kirima Nagi, in the flesh, standing smack dab in the middle of the white room, nodding at him.

"S-sempai, what's going…?" He didn't need to finish. The moment he asked, he noticed the unlit cigarette in her hand. "That's…!"

"Yeah, well, you know how it is," she said, making no effort to hide it.

"They caught you, didn't they? But why…and in a place like this?"

"Whatever," Nagi gave him a half grin. It made quite an impact. It was this sort of impression that had made him fall in love with her in the first place.

"Sempai, um…" he tried to talk further.

She cut him off. "Sorry again about that other thing. I still think it's better for you this way."

"Oh, no, that's…"

"Oh, hey, you were 1-D, weren't you?"

"Yeah…"

"Were you friends with Kusatsu Akiko?"

Masami thought his heart was going to leap out of his mouth.

"Er, n-not really…" he mumbled.

Nagi glared at him. "You knew her?"

"I went out with her once."

"On a date?"

"No! I mean, uh, it was like…" he said, scrambling to form a coherent sentence

Nagi looked at his face, and grinned again. "Not what I'm asking. You notice her acting weird lately?"

"Well, yeah, I guess so."

"How long?"

"Maybe…two or three weeks?"

"Matches up…" Nagi whispered to herself.

Masami felt a shiver run down his spine, but he didn't let it show.

"Matches what?"

"Mm? Oh, never mind," Nagi said evasively.

"Something happen to Kusatsu? If there's anything I can do to help, sempai…" he pressed.

"Nah, it's nothing important."

"Of course it's important. I mean, *this* is deliberate, isn't it?" he said, taking the cigarette out of Nagi's hand.

"Hey, Saotome-kun," Nagi said, troubled.

"It's something big enough that you're deliberately getting yourself suspended, isn't it? Let me tell the teachers."

"They won't do anything! Teachers are nothing but wage slaves," she said coldly.

Masami couldn't argue with that. He had suggested it precisely because he had the same opinion. If they left things up to the teachers, everything would be forgotten in no time.

"Then…" he persisted.

Nagi took his hand and held it tightly.

"Thanks, but no. You're normal, and you shouldn't have anything to do with this."

"But…" he said as three male teachers came stomping into the ladies room.

"You again!" they shouted at Nagi.

Nagi was unaffected.

"Um…" Masami tried talking to them, but they didn't even look at him. One of them took the cigarette out of his hand, and said, "This is evidence!" thrusting it out towards Nagi.

She said nothing.

She was hauled off to the guidance office like a wanted criminal.

Masami followed after her, looking worried, but one of the teachers told him to go back to his room, so he simply watched them leave.

There was nobody else around, and the color on his face slowly faded.

"............."

From down the hall, he heard the office door slam open. All Masami could do is turn and walk away. There was no emotion left on his face.

"............."

Nagi's choice of words kept echoing through his mind. She had said, "Matches up." All he could think was that it matched up to the first girl who had 'run away,' Suzumiya Takako.

Nagi knew something.

Something too close for comfort.

"............."

His mask cracked for just a second, letting out a glimpse of his true face underneath.

His eyes were withered, inhuman, like a man who has just wandered in the desert for a week with no water and let sand creep into every pore on his body.

5.

"**K**irima Nagi? Why would she?!" cried out Yurihara when she heard Masami's story. They were in the pool changing rooms where thankfully nobody ever dared to come inside during winter.

"I don't know. But she's clearly caught wind of something."

Masami told Yurihara about Nagi six days into her suspension. During that period, he was stalking the girls that they had planned next to entrap and kill. It quickly became obvious that Nagi was taking them down one after the other—all of Kusatsu Akiko's Junior High school friends. Today, he'd seen her attack Kinoshita Kyoko, and make her promise never to take drugs again.

In the shadows of the school, it was clear that she was playing out some sort of hero fantasy of her own.

"Why?! We did everything right!" Yurihara cried out hysterically.

"Yes, we did. Which is why she hasn't caught wind of us yet," he said quietly. But inside, he knew just how precarious of a position that they were in. If they had been just a little bit late in disposing of Kusatsu Akiko, Nagi would most certainly have deduced what was wrong with her. It had been a very close shave.

"We can't kill anyone else from Shinyo Academy. We don't want her suspecting that you're a student here."

"Why don't we just kill her?" Yurihara suggested.

"Not yet. I don't know how much she knows or how she found out. we need to know that at least."

"She needs to die! We won't leave any evidence behind! And she's crazy; nobody'll notice when she vanishes."

It was obvious that they were in the same class. Yurihara knew Nagi all too well.

"But her current parents are very rich. And she's got several hundred million yen in the bank. She disappears, and I guarantee you that it won't be put down as a runaway. When money gets involved, there's no telling who'll come out of the woodwork. That's how human society works."

Yurihara remained silent. She looked at the floor, bit her lip, and then whispered petulantly, "...Is that the only reason?"

"Eh?"

"Is that the only reason you won't kill Kirima Nagi? There's another reason, isn't there?"

"What are you talking about?"

"Saotome-kun, don't lie to me. You're in love with her, aren't you?"

Masami looked away.

"Wh-why do you think that?"

"Am I wrong? I'm right, aren't I?" she asked as she looked up and glared at him.

"I…" Masami started to say, when suddenly…

"—what are you doing in here, Echoes?" a cheery girl's voice asked, as the door to the changing room swung open.

From the stripes on her uniform, it was clear that she was third year. And a bright and sunny girl at that.

"Uh, oops? My mistake, sorry!" she said, scratching her head.

"Ah! D-don't—!" Masami yelled, pretending that the girl had caught them in the middle of a romantic moment. It was okay, though. She hadn't overheard them.

"Sorry! Sorry! You two have fun now!" she commented smiling. She was clearly blushing from embarrassment as she started to duck back out the door.

But at that moment, Yurihara's body shot forward like a bullet. She let out a hiss like a king cobra, and sank her teeth into the back of the third year girl's neck.

There was a sharp cracking sound.

"W-wha?!" cried Masami, trying to get between them, but he was already too late. She had bitten through the girl's spine, killing her instantly. It was over before the girl even realized what was happening to her.

"What the hell were you thinking?! I just told you not to kill at school!" Masami yelled, turning on Yurihara.

But when he saw her face, his manner changed.

She was as white as a sheet and shivering violently. "H-how…how is *he* here?" she whimpered with her latest victim's blood splattered across her mouth.

"What do you mean?"

"Him! Echoes! He's here!"

"Who or what is Echoes?"

"My 'original'! The over-evolved man!" She hugged her hands to her chest, but that didn't stop her shaking.

"C-calm down! You can explain later. First, we have to get rid of this body!" Masami yelled, glancing down at the girl's corpse. Looking closely, he recognized her face. "She's…Kamikishiro Naoko?"

She was one of Nagi's few precious friends. That's why he knew her. Nagi had taken a year off in Junior High due to illness, but she had been in the same class as Kamikishiro at the time.

(Why is Nagi's friend…? Is this just a coincidence? No, it can't be…)

He felt the last piece fall into place. Just as they had disposed of Kusatsu Akiko in the nick of time, once again Fate had given them a desperately needed chance.

"Don't worry, Manticore. The advantage is on our side." He smiled, and gently put his arms around her trembling shoulders.

"Eh?" she questioned as she looked up, and was greeted with a warm and knowing nod and a luminous smile.

***

They carried Kamikishiro Naoko's body to a secret room in the basement. Yurihara leaned over the corpse and began disposing of the evidence.

As he watched, Masami grinned.

(I'll make sure you live through this. I promise. Whatever

happens to me…it'll be worth it.)

A single line of a song ran through Saotome Masami's mind.

For some reason, it was not a song by his beloved group The Doors. He had forgotten the exact name of it. It was just a song that he had overheard somewhere and barely remembered. He couldn't even remember the whole line; just a snippet echoing through his mind like a broken record.

It was a song by a band that wasn't anywhere near as famous as The Doors; they were a freak band called Oingo Boingo that were famous for their weirded-out tunes. The name of the song was "No One Lives Forever."

The pop, cheery tune didn't match the sinister name, nor the blood-ridden lyrics. Masami began singing under his breath.

"…No one, no one, no one, no one, no one no

one no one no one no one no one no one no one no one no
one no one no one no one no one no one no one no one no
one no one no one no one no one no one no one no one no
one no one no one no one no one no one no one no one no
one no one…"

His smile continued till the rest of the phrase, "lives forever," came back to him. The smile contained more than the radiance of one prepared to sacrifice his life for the object of his affections—there was a hint of evil and of deeply personal pleasure to it.

In front of him came a sound like wind whistling through a crack in the wall as the man-eater consumed the girl.

Chapter Four
I Wish You Heaven

Kimura Akio
second year, class B

1.

"Kamikishiro Naoko is dead. You should forget about her," was all that was written in the letter. It looked like a computer print out.

"What?" I picked up the envelope and studied it for a moment, but all it had listed on it was my name, "Kimura Akio" and home address. There was no return address at all, and judging from the stamp, it had been posted in the same town where I attended high school.

At first, I thought it must be a prank by one of my old classmates. My little fling with Kamikishiro Naoko kinda became public knowledge after it ended.

But it seemed a little late for that. Two full years had passed since I'd last seen her, and it was a little late for this kind of prank.

Still, she vanished abruptly during my second year, and I still don't know why she disappeared. I don't think anybody knows. Did anybody ever really know what she was thinking?

***

Kamikishiro Naoko and I first hooked up in a pretty strange kinda way.

This all took place not too long after the spring term had begun.

I was smoking a Caster Mild around the back of the school one day at lunch, when a boy and a girl showed up. Luckily for me, I was hiding behind a tree, so they didn't see me.

There was kind of a long, meaningful silence, so I took that opportunity to hide even better, hoping to get an eyeful.

But they barely even looked at each other, they just sort of stood there, fidgeting.

(Ah ha…)

Just as I got it figured out, the girl opened her mouth. "Did you…read the letter?" she said, clasping her hands.

"Mm," he said evasively.

The whole thing was kinda old fashioned, and I was just about to lose interest, when the boy suddenly looked around nervously and asked, "You are alone…right?"

"Hunh?" she blinked. And so did I. Most people usually come alone at moments like this. Of course, there are some losers that need their friends to goad them on.

"So you're not gonna beat me up or something?" he asked, relieved.

What, was this kid afraid of girls or something?

Then I finally noticed.

His slippers were blue, and hers were yellow. Our school has it set up so that each grade has a different color. I was wearing green ones. The boy was a first year, and the girl was third year.

"No, nothing like that!" she exclaimed. The moment that I knew she was my *sempai,* she started looking extremely grown up…and hot. I'm pretty picky when it comes to girls, but I could tell she had on makeup that subtly made her eyes look bigger. But it was natural makeup, so that the teachers would never notice. It was also obvious that she worked pretty hard at making herself always look cheerful.

But the other one, this first year kid, looked like a child. He was a baby-faced pretty boy, but kinda ordinary. But hey, some girls are into that.

"Then what is it?" he asked the older girl vacantly.

"You know…" she said, turning red and staring at her feet. Her expression clearly showed that it wasn't anything but what it was.

(Hunh…)

But I also knew how the kid felt. He couldn't figure out *why*. Why was this pretty senior asking a kid like him out? It was natural to be dubious instead of happy.

Course now I'm in college, I know loads of girls who have boyfriends younger than them. But that just doesn't happen in high school. Up to high school, you're in a sort of unmistakable feudal system. A girl could date a college guy or a Junior High kid or anyone she wanted to outside of school, but there was an unwritten rule that she could only date boys her year or older on the inside.

"Um…Kamikishiro-san?" he asked, very troubled. This is where I learned her name.

"What?" she replied, looking at him with a mixture of anxiety and expectation. Men find this kind of look hard to say no to.

But he was looking away and didn't see it.

"I'm sorry! I just can't do this!" he sort of shrieked as he turned and ran away.

"Ah…!" Kamikishiro almost chased after him, but stopped herself. Her shoulders slumped.

From behind, I could see her head hung down and a little sideways. Somehow, this angle made her all the more beautiful, like some sort of female Don Quixote, fighting the invisible school rules. Gotta say, it impressed the shit out of me.

While I was off feeling all impressed, she suddenly rolled her head around like an old man getting out of the bath.

"Not again," she said exhaustedly, and then spun round and looked right at me.

I didn't have time to hide. Our eyes met.

"Enjoy the show? Ah ha ha!" she laughed, and strolled over to me. She'd known that I was there the whole time.

"Uh, n-no. I-I didn't mean to watch," I said, scrambling.

She reached out her hand, and said, "My fee," as she pulled a Caster Mild out of my pocket. "Damn, I've been dying for a nicotine hit all day."

She stuck the cigarette between her lips and looked at me expectantly. I hurriedly lit it.

"Pretty smooth," she said with a smirk. She let out a big puff of smoke. Her manner was the polar opposite of a moment before.

But looking at her profile, I could make out the tear tracks.

"You were serious," I said, expecting her to deny it and move on.

But instead, she just nodded and said, "You bet I was."
She slumped into a crouch and continued, "Serious as I've
ever been." She hugged her knees to her chest and buried her
face in her skirt.

"Why can't we pick who we fall in love with? It would be
so much easier…" she said forlornly.

"Well, yeah, true, but frankly, I think you're better off
getting rejected by a guy like that," I said in a very honest
tone.

She looked up. Her tears had made her eyeliner run a bit.
Unexpectedly, she said, "…Don't."

"What?"

"Don't be nice to me. I don't want to fall for you too."

"*What?!*" I yelped, completely off balance now. She stood
up, no longer crying, and smiled. "Just kidding. But you're a
good guy. So, what's your name?"

"Kimura, 2-B."

"I'm Kamikishiro, 3-F. You planning on going to class this
afternoon?"

"Not really." I had Modern Japanese and Political Science
left, but I was planning on skipping them.

"Then I'll buy you a MOS Burger. You know, pay you
back for cheering me up. C'mon, I know a way out the back,"
she winked naughtily.

And that's basically how we got started.

That's pretty much what we were like the whole time. We
were never really 'in love,' as such. We might have looked
like we were from the outside or something, but she never
really fell for me. At least, I don't think she did. That was two
years ago.

2.

Eventually, Kamikishiro did convince that first year kid—his name was Tanaka Shiro—into going out with her. When she attacked, no one could stop her.

One time, I just had to tell her, "I just don't know what you see in him."

She often called me up and asked me to hang out with her.

Yeah, you could call it a date. We'd watch movies, eat out, shoot pool and bet money on the game. We'd also do other stuff too, but you know how it is.

"Well, you see…he's an archer."

"An archer? On the archery team?"

If I remember it correctly, we were on one of those slow moving ferris wheels at an amusement park. It was like a picture postcard of those cheesy high school dates that you see in manga.

"Yeah. First time I saw him, he was still in Junior High and was in some contest. You ever seen one? They all line up and shoot. The first one to miss loses. It was pretty damn cool.

He did pretty well, but eventually lost. But his eyes…when he stared at that tiny little target so far away there was this glitter in them. Gave me goosebumps. And then, he'd let the arrow fly…and swoosh!"

"Sounds kinda shallow…" I said, somewhat disgusted. All that had nothing whatsoever to do with Tanaka himself or with his personality. Of course, he'd be reluctant.

"I'd much rather play around with someone like you, *Kimu*-kun. You're more fun. And I got no plans to take up archery myself. But I can't shake the feeling that kid is meant for bigger things."

"And I'm not, you mean? Ouch," I grimaced. The words 'someone like you' made things crystal clear. Nothing I could do when she put it that way.

"Yep. You're like me that way. I'm a mess. And, frankly, so are you, *Kimu*-kun."

"Can't deny that," I said, chuckling. It was true. If it wasn't, then why would I be dating a girl who I knew full well had another guy on the side? Still, I was falling for her pretty hard by this point. Yet I never even considered trying to get her to break things off with Tanaka. It wasn't just a mess, either. It was a freaking train wreck just waiting to happen. And on top of that, she was hardly the only girl I was seeing. Yeah, we were exactly the same.

"I'll be honest. *Shiro*-kun doesn't get me at all," she said, sighing bitterly. "He tries not to hurt me, but he always talks kinda standoffish, and that just hurts me more. He just doesn't get that at all."

"Huh. Can't say I do either."

"I'm just getting in his way. I don't think he really needs to be in love yet."

Sometimes, I found her nearly impossible to understand.

It's easy to do the typical guy thing and just bitch that girls are all complicated and stuff, but her level of complexity was clearly at a notch or two above the other girls her age. I'm pretty sure most of them wouldn't have been able to follow her either. As it was, the only friends that I knew she had were me and some girl in her class called Kirima Nagi. That girl was even weirder than Kamikishiro, so I guess that's why they got along. Truthfully, Kirima was better looking than Kamikishiro, but I always did like Kamikishiro better. Even now.

"But do the two of us need it? I guess so. Feels like I'm kinda incomplete on my own, you know?"

"That's it exactly! See, we're the same," she gave me a tiny smile, leaned forward, and put her lips on mine.

It was no big deal. It was not exactly the first time we'd kissed.

"…you do that with Tanaka?" I asked curtly.

"Hell, no," she grinned, denying it instantly.

She was always at her most attractive when she wasn't outright trying to be sexy or to act cute. I never figured out why.

***

I was pretty sure that the letter was a prank, but something about it just kept bugging me. I decided to skip class and head over to the town where I'd gone to high school. Call it a hunch, but whoever had sent the letter probably lived there.

My family still lives there, but I didn't swing by; I just headed straight for Shinyo Academy. I didn't think any of the current students were behind it, but my legs took me in that direction anyway.

"Ah! Akio! Over here!" someone called as I waited for the bus to arrive.

I turned around and found a girl who'd been in my same class during my first and third years—Miyashita Touka. The first thing that I noticed was the huge Spalding bag over her shoulder.

"Hey, what's up?" I replied.

"What're you doing back here? It's not even New Year's yet!" Miyashita was a cute girl, but I'd never made a pass at her—which is probably why we were still friends.

"Yeah, no reason in particular. You?"

"You didn't hear? I failed exams. I'm a *ronin*. On my way to cram school as we speak."

"Oh, right."

"Yep. Guess you forgot all about us when you moved up, huh?"

"You sound bitter. Fighting with that designer boyfriend of yours?" I asked, knowing that she'd been dating an older boy in that line of work since her second year.

"Do not even talk to me about *him*. He never even calls!" she said, pouting.

"He's probably trying not to disrupt your studies."

"Nah, he studies more than me. He's trying to get some sort of award. Makes me sick."

"Hmmm…"

"What about you? Got a college girl yet?"

I made a face. "Nope."

"Aw, that third year girl still dragging you back?"

"She was a third year then. She'd be twenty now."

"You're…you're counting her birthdays? She dumped you and vanished! Give up on her already!"

"It's none of your business," I spat.

She looked pissed, but she grabbed my hand.

"W-what?"

"Come with me. *We* are having *tea*."

Still pissed, she dragged me into a nearby café by the name of Tristan.

"What about cram school?"

"Screw it. I'm gonna fail again this year anyway," she said recklessly.

She plunked herself down in a booth and shouted at the counter, "Two American coffees!" She then turned on me to tell me exactly what I already knew, "You're an *idiot*."

"I know," I replied petulantly.

"No, you don't! You think you're some sort of hero, don't you? What with that mess two years ago," Miyashita announced. She'd always been like this, sort of self-righteous and inclined to stick her nose into everything.

"I do not. That was just…"

"It wasn't you, was it? Her lover. You didn't even know who it was you were taking the fall for, did you?"

"………"

Two years ago, after Kamikishiro had vanished, they found a blanket, pillow and electric heater in a storage room near the gym, where nobody ever went. It was obvious somebody had snuck into the school and had been living there. At first, they thought it was a drifter, but then they found an accessory that had belonged to Kamikishiro (according to one of the girls in her class), and it turned into a student body scandal.

I don't know what kind of people Kamikishiro's parents were, but their daughter had disappeared and the school suspected her involvement in illicit activities, yet the parents made no protest at all to the accusations. In her continued absence, the school made preparations to forcibly expel her. At which point, a certain male student announced that he'd been her lover, and all hell broke loose after that.

"She didn't bring any outsiders into the school. Don't expel her," he'd said.

The teachers didn't even pretend to believe him. But the students made a huge fuss about it and just to calm things down, the school suspended the boy and relented on Kamikishiro's punishment.

But Kamikishiro never did show up again. Her name was even kicked off the rosters at graduation, due to a lack of credits.

It all amounted to nothing in the end. There was never really anything to the story. As a result of the commotion, the boy got his comeuppance, though. He received a series of Dear John letters from all of his many girlfriends, telling him that he was a loser and that they were dumping his sorry ass.

"...No, I knew who Kamikishiro was seeing," I told Miyashita with a faint smile.

"Liar."

"No, really."

"Then, who? Who'd she drop you for?"

"An alien. He took her with him back into space."

No sooner were the words out of my mouth than a slap echoed through the café. Miyashita had belted me one across the face.

"Get a grip on yourself! Be a man, and just move on!" she said, furious.

Wasn't like she had any special feelings for me, mind you. She was just that kind of girl.

"S-sorry," I said, rubbing my cheek sheepishly.

But I hadn't been joking. That was exactly what Kamikishiro had said to me.

3.

"**K**imu-kun, do you think human existence is justified?" Kamikishiro asked, out of the blue one day.

"Nope," I said, instantly. I was getting used to her non-sequitors.

"Dang, neither do I," she sighed.

We were lying next to each other on the bank of the river that ran along the road leading up to school. Since most of the students took the bus, people hardly ever walked along this road. It was already dark out, and we could see stars above us.

"Humans just aren't that great. However much our civilization advances, we can't seem to do anything to make ourselves happier," I said, obviously, trying to impress her with something profound.

"Yeah...maybe," she replied. She seemed kinda serious.

"Why do you ask?"

"I just met this guy, but..."

"You in love again? What about Tanaka?" I asked, surprised.

"Yeah. Yeah, I am, but let's put that aside for a moment," she said, sitting up. She gazed at the wavering reflection of the city lights on the moving water of the river. "He's from outer space."

She looked serious. She had to be joking, but she didn't seem to be waiting for me to laugh, so I took it as some sort of metaphor, and just nodded. "Mm-hmm."

"But I don't think he's from some other planet. It's like, in space there's this big consciousness, and it sent him here to, you know, 'test mankind' or something. Kinda like the inspection robots that always show up in Hoshi Shinichi's short stories? But he's not a machine or anything. It's just that his body isn't something that exists on Earth. It can, like, turn into anything. So, when he landed on earth, he disguised himself as human and tried to examine the world, but there were a few mistakes, and he didn't quite manage to pull off being human quite right."

"…………"

"He's evolved a little too much. He's got more power within him than any human will ever have in a thousand years—no, in ten thousand years! Apparently, space is just so big that they couldn't match him up with Earth time just right, so his true nature came out ahead of time, and the government or some kind of big corporation got a hold of him. But the idiots thought that he was just some mutant, and they did all sorts of experiments on him and cloned him. But, unlike him, that cloned copy turned into a brutal man-eater."

I no longer had the foggiest idea what she was talking about. I elected to keep quiet until I could pick up the thread again.

"He wanted to communicate all this, but he couldn't. He

was programmed in such a way that he couldn't talk to humans directly. It was so that he wouldn't reveal his true identity to anyone. Which was fine. I mean, after all, he was sent here to test humans and see if they would be nice to him. He wasn't here to negotiate or make speeches or anything. He was just here to observe, so they named him Echoes, since all he can do is reflect back the words that people spoke to him."

"............."

"But the man-eater killed everyone in the research facility and escaped. Now, it's off hiding inside of human society somewhere. But Echoes came after it, and he...and he met me."

"What's he gonna do if he catches it?"

"Fight it, I guess. If he doesn't, it'll just take over the world or something."

"But he's an alien. Why does he care what happens here?"

"Yeah, true...basically, he's just nice."

"That's it?"

"Isn't it enough? Isn't niceness the best motivation that someone can have?" she asked, looking at me kinda solemn. She then let out a sigh. "Half of this is just me reading between the lines. I think he's got some sort of other complicated reason too. You know, something about maintaining the balance of the planet. But if that was all...its kinda sad, don't you think?" she whispered pretty downcast. She looked on the verge of tears, which made me uncomfortable.

I felt the kind of tightness in my chest that I thought that I'd left behind in Junior High.

I cleared my throat to hide this feeling, and said deliberately rough, "So, how the hell did this Echoes guy even explain all of this to you? I thought he couldn't talk?" It was a stupid nitpick.

So she said, "Ah ha ha! You're too smart! I can't fool you," and cackled.

"That's all?" I asked. The story was a bit too detailed to be dismissed like this.

"Yep, I was just kidding. Stupid little fairy tale—" Kamikishiro said with an impish grin stealing over the corners of her mouth.

We sat in silence for a while.

She was the first to break the silence. "But if Echoes wins, he'll probably go back to his home in the stars."

"Sounds romantic to me. Kinda like the *tanabata* festival."

"I wonder what he'll tell them about us humans. I don't suppose there's much chance of him saying, 'Don't worry, they're a good species,' is there?"

"Where is he now?"

"Hiding at the school. Don't tell anyone."

I laughed. "Don't worry, I won't."

Stupid promise.

Because of that promise, I got myself suspended and had to lower my ambitions for college. But since I turned all my friends into enemies and spent the rest of school isolated, I had nothing to do but study, and eventually, I used my grades to make up for the poor conduct report.

"The stars are so far away," Kamikishiro said, gazing up at the night sky.

"They're farther away than our lives," I said. I'm not sure what her story really meant, but she'd managed to get the answer that she'd wanted out of me, as I told her, "But if you open your heart to Echoes, then I'm sure he'll learn to like humanity."

"You think so?"

"I want to think so. Because the story you told me leaves us no salvation."

"Yeah. I hope you're right," she said, turning towards me and smiling.

But at the time, I didn't want her to smile. I wanted her to get angry with me for saying something so stupid. I tried to think of something even stupider to say, but instead we headed back home. I walked off down the road to the station, and she went back towards the school, saying that she'd take the bus.

That's the last time I ever saw her.

She didn't come to school the next day. Or the day after that. She never came again.

***

Two cups of American coffee appeared in front of Miyashita Touka and me. Miyashita picked up on the waitress' look of keen interest and cooled down a little.

"Sorry, I shouldn't have slapped you. Still…" she said in a hushed tone.

"Don't worry. I know. I'm an idiot."

"I really do think that you need to let her go. She's…what was her name?"

"Kamikishiro Naoko."

"Oh, right. I didn't know her very well, but I think if she really did like you, Akio, that she'd want you to move on now. That's why she didn't say anything when she left. Make sense?"

"That…that'd be nice."

Truth is, I'm pretty sure she never thought twice about me.

Eventually, Miyashita Touka let me go, forcibly exhorting me to cheer up.

We parted at the door to the coffee shop.

"Take care. You know, you really ought to do something about that hero complex of yours. Gonna get you into trouble someday. You've got tests to study for."

"I guess," she said with her head to one side. "But still…"

"Suit yourself," I said, turning to leave. It was then that she called after me.

"—Kimura-kun!"

I looked back and nearly tripped over my own feet.

It was certainly Miyashita Touka standing there, but for some reason, I felt like I was looking at a completely different person—a boy. It was as if she'd transformed or something.

"Wh-what?"

"Kamikishiro Naoko performed her duty admirably. You should perform your own duty, and make her proud. That's the only thing you can do for her," she proclaimed like she was giving some speech on stage.

Then she spun on her heel and was lost in the crowd.

"…………"

I stared after her, watching the crowd flow onwards.

***

When my bus reached the stop in front of Shinyo Academy, it was already past sunset, and there were no students in sight. Apparently, even the sports teams gave up on

practice and called it a day, once it got dark. This must be why none of our teams has ever even so much as qualified for the national tournaments. It hadn't changed a bit since I was last there.

The gates were closed. Outsiders had to identify themselves over an intercom to get in, so I passed right by them.

I entered the school through a gap between the fences that Kamikishiro had shown me.

The darkened school grounds were silent like an abandoned building. The towering school building looked kinda like a giant, looming tombstone.

Until about a year before, I had actually come here every day. But now, I was a stranger.

Not much that I can say that was good about my years in high school, but I felt a pain in my chest when I thought about how little connection that I had now to my past. I remember Kamikishiro, and the abuse that I took after the incident like it was yesterday, but the rest of it was all far too long ago.

".........."

Why did I come here? If I was looking for the source of the letter, this place wasn't going to be of any use.

But this high school was the only remaining connection that I had with Kamikishiro. Someone else had moved into her apartment. There were no traces of her left.

There was nowhere else for me to go.

She just wasn't here.

Yeah. Somewhere inside, I had wondered if Kamikishiro herself had sent the letter.

But that was probably wrong. Even here in school, she wasn't around. The letter was nothing but a prank.

Everything was over. It was all in the past.

"………"

I looked up at the sky. It was cloudy, and I couldn't see the stars. And yet, I felt like I could see them like I had when I used to lay with her on the river bank.

She had told me all of her secrets, metaphorically. Told *me*; not Tanaka Shiro, not anyone else. And I never understood what she meant by it.

Wasn't that enough? That's all the reason I needed to love her for the rest of my life. No matter how much I fell in love with some other girl, she will always live inside of me in the way that she was then—impossible to understand, and more than a little crazy.

"Life is brief, young maiden, fall in love."

I whispered a snatch of the gondola song that she always used to sing while I wandered around the school.

I found myself in front of the gym. Suddenly, I wanted to see the storage room where the interloper had hidden himself. Their exact relationship remained a mystery, but it was the last known trace of her.

I grabbed a flashlight from the emergency supplies, and shone it around the gym. I had forgotten half of the features of the place. Guess I really wanted to forget all about high school.

I found some kind of door or cover or something down by the floor, near the main entrance. Figured that must be it. So I hunkered down and opened it.

It was just an empty space. Iron pillars, concrete floor, bare ceiling. The foundations of the gym, I guess. Designed to absorb the impact of an earthquake.

I'd been here three years and never known it was here.

(Guess this isn't it…)

I turned to leave.

But something moved near my foot.

There was a dry rustle.

"Mm…?"

I shone the light at my feet.

There was something black and dried. I thought it was a glove at first, maybe forgotten by a workman, but it was too thin for that.

It wasn't meant to be put on over a hand. *It was a hand.*

"………"

I stared at it in shock for a moment…then screamed.

It was a mummified human hand.

(W-w-w-w-what the hell is this?!)

My knees gave out and I fell on my ass.

When Kamikishiro had vanished, she hadn't been the only one. A number of other students had vanished both before and after her.

I'd never connected them before…but I could think of no other reason why a hand would be lying on the floor of the school.

Maybe it was because I'd kicked it or maybe it was the exposure to the outside air, whichever the case, the hand crumbled away to dust before my very eyes. And within seconds, there was nothing left of it at all.

(What does it mean? What the hell happened here two years ago?)

But there was nothing to give me those answers. There

was nothing for me to do but sit there in the dark, shuddering in fear…

Chapter Five
Heartbreaker

Niitoki Kei
second year, class F

1.

"**K**ei, there's a first year boy asking for you," my classmate Mishima said.

I looked up from my book and asked, "Who?"

"Dunno. But he's cute. Tch, the discipline committee president, eating all the young boys…" she cackled.

I gave her a pained smile, stood up, and went into the hall.

When he saw me, he bowed his head politely. "Niitoki-sempai? I'm Tanaka Shiro, 1-D."

"Tanaka-kun? You wanted to see me?"

"You were on the gate this morning, weren't you?"

One of the duties of the discipline committee members, which we all took turns doing, was to stand at the gate and monitor the students coming in and out.

"Yeah. What about it?"

"Did you see 3-F's Kamikishiro-san arrive?"

"Naoko-san? I know her, but no, she didn't come today. But she's nearly always late…"

"She's not in class either," he said gravely.

"Really? Must be skipping."

"No," he said, quite sure of himself. "Recently, she had some sort of reason why she had to come to school everyday."

(Is this kid in love with her…?)

Seemed like it. Maybe he was gonna ask her out today.

"Hunh. I don't know. If she's not here, ask her tomorrow."

"That might be too late!" he exclaimed anxiously. "You really don't know anything?!"

"You call her house?"

"There's never anyone there."

"Eh?"

"Her parents are in the middle of an ugly divorce. Her mother's gone to her parents' house, and her father never comes home."

"Really?"

"Everyone in the apartment building's talking about it. Everybody I asked told me all about it."

"Hunh…" I said.

Suddenly, a voice cut in from the side. "You should ask Kirima Nagi."

Both of us swung around in surprise. My *kouhai* on the discipline committee, Saotome-kun, was standing there.

"Masami? What do you…?" Tanaka-kun said, wide eyed. Later, I found out these two were in the same class.

"I was just passing by; happened to overhear. Thought you might like to know."

"Know what?"

"I don't know any details, but Kamikishiro Naoko-sempai and Kirima Nagi have been friends since Junior High. She's just off of suspension, so she might know something about Kamikishiro-sempai."

I blinked. It was the first I'd heard of Naoko-san being friends with the legendary Kirima Nagi from the class next door. And here I thought I knew about most people in the school.

"How do you know that?" I asked Saotome.

"Oh, I asked Kirima Nagi out once. Picked up a few things back then."

"You asked her out?!"

It took guts to even talk to the Fire Witch. I'll give him that.

"She said no," he admitted.

"What class is this Kirima person in?" Tanaka-kun asked forcibly. Somehow, he'd never heard of her.

"Second year, class D. Right next door."

"Okay!"

"W-whoa, hold on there! No telling what'll happen if you just burst in on her!" I said as if she were some sort of lion. But it was true. She'd punched out one boy's front teeth before.

I couldn't let them go alone, so I followed them to class D. I asked a girl I knew near the door. "Ah, Suema-san. Is Kirima-san here? I've got a first year boy who wants to talk to her…"

"She's not here today."

"Really? She came in the gate." I knew my words to be true. I was on the gate. I'd seen her arrive.

"So, she is here? I haven't seen her come to class, though," Suema-san said, shrugging.

We looked at each other.

"What…what's going on?" Saotome-kun asked.

"Sounds like she *is* involved," Tanaka-kun said in a shrill voice.

"Hmmm…" I was seriously worried myself now. Naoko-san and Kirima Nagi…what were they up to?

As we stood there in front of the door, someone asked, "Could I get in here?" We turned around to find Yurihara Minako, the best student in the school, standing right before us.

"Oh, sorry," Saotome-kun said, moving aside.

She nodded, and strode regally into the room like some sort of queen.

The bell rang, so we all split up and headed back to our respective rooms.

***

"Naoko's vanished. I can't find her anywhere," Kirima Nagi said in a place steeped in shadows.

The man with her said nothing. His expression never wavered. Nagi grew irritated at his lack of reaction, and shook her head violently.

"I called her cell, but she didn't answer. You don't know anything?" she pressed on.

The man was unable to talk, so he simply shook his head slowly.

"She may have gotten caught in *its* net. That thing Naoko said was your sibling."

"…………" The man did not respond.

Kirima Nagi scowled at him. Finally, she spat, "We should never have listened to you. We should have just called the cops, or the Self-Defense Force. If the world knew about *it*, it would've just washed its hands of the whole business and vanished to some place where we couldn't follow. But if Naoko's dead, then we're already too late…"

She buried her hands in her face, her nail digging into her cheeks and forehead.

"............"

The man didn't move.

"Say something! You talked to Naoko, didn't you?! Try and let me know what you're thinking!" Kirima Nagi shouted, grabbing his collar. It was a Brooks Brothers cotton shirt that Kamikishiro Naoko had bought for him.

"............" Even when she shook him roughly, he did nothing but stare back at her in silence.

"God damn it! I *will* find you, Manticore!" she howled, uncharacteristically angry. "And you're gonna help, Echoes!"

He nodded. But, yes, there was something remote about that motion.

As if he were monitoring Nagi's reactions.

***

It bugged the hell out of me, so I took gate duty again that day after school. In the morning, we had to check the cards as they went through, but on the way home, the job was simply boring.

"You are nosy," laughed the first year kid who should have been on duty. He gave up his place happily.

Nosy?

I guess so.

There's a part of me that can't stand to see something unclear, something uncertain. That part of me wants to fix those things. Once when I was at a friend's house, they left me alone in their room with a half-done jigsaw puzzle, and when they came back, I had already finished it. They were pretty angry too.

The reason that I was on the unpopular discipline committee, and the president of it, no less, was simply because of this "clarity impulse" of mine.

"Anyone?" "Who wants to do it?" they'd all ask, but nobody ever raised their hand. They just sat there in silence. And before I knew it, my hand was up.

It's like a disease, I know.

With Naoko-san missing, if I hadn't been asked, I'd never have gotten involved, but now that I had been, I wouldn't be able to sleep until I'd cleared things up.

My friends tell me, "You're like a big sister. There's just something reliable about you," which I took as a compliment (though, they may have been making fun of me.) But the truth is, it's just my neurosis.

(Talking to the Fire Witch is scary, but if I don't, I can't settle down!)

But even when most of the students had gone home, and the sky was starting to darken, Kirima Nagi had yet to appear.

It was well past the time when the gate guard was free to go home, and I was starting to wonder what else I could do, when Tanaka-kun and Saotome-kun came up.

"Ah, sempai! Did Kirima Nagi go home?" Saotome-kun asked.

"No, not yet."

"Oh," said Tanaka-kun, hanging his head.

"Why don't we look for her together? I'm sure she's still in the school somewhere," I suggested.

"That's what we were going to do," Tanaka-kun nodded. "We were talking about it in the classroom."

"I'm a little worried about Kirima Nagi," Saotome-kun said. She may have rejected him, but it seemed that he still liked her.

"But where do you think she is?"

"Somewhere where nobody would notice her...on the roof, or maybe under the gym? Oh, or the pool changing rooms..." Saotome-kun suggested.

"Why would she be in a place like that?" Tanaka-kun said in an irritated voice.

"I don't know. But everyone knows her, so she must be someplace like that, or somebody would've noticed."

"Let's check them out," I said, and we headed back into the eerily quiet school.

***

While on our way to the roof, I couldn't help but ask, "Tanaka-kun, were you and Naoko-san...?"

"Um," he said, worried.

"Kamikishiro-sempai asked him out," Saotome-kun interjected.

"What?!" I yelped.

"Masami! That was a secret!"

"Don't worry, *sempai* won't tell."

I was still reeling as they spoke. "You're joking, right?"

"I certainly thought so. I kept asking her if it was a joke, but she kept saying that she was serious."

"Hunh..." I stared at his face closely.

"Please don't tell anyone."

"Okay, I won't. But still..."

"It was pretty confusing, but I couldn't think of a reason to say no, so I ended up going out with her."

"But I could swear that Naoko-san had a different boyfriend..."

"Yeah, she does. Second year guy named Kimura Akio. Never really worked up the nerve to ask about that…"

"Kimura? He picked up Naoko-san too? But it can't be too serious with a guy like that…"

Kimura-kun was from the class next to mine, and he was an infamous playboy. Legend had it that he'd made a pass at every second year girl in the entire school. He'd even flirted with me— the discipline committee president!

"Maybe, maybe not. Either way, I was never able to figure out what she really wanted."

"Do you like Naoko-san?"

"D-do I?"

"Be clear," my fixation popped right up and out of my mouth.

"If we're going to the roof, the fire escape round back is better," Saotome-kun said, glancing around us.

"Why?"

"The door's locked, isn't it?"

"Oh, right."

As we went round the back, we saw somebody coming down the fire escape.

"Ah…!"

We chased after them, but they were gone before we could get there. But they were tall, and probably male, so we didn't chase them any further. Whoever it was had headed towards the gates and was probably going home.

"If he was up there, than Kirima Nagi probably isn't."

"Yeah. Let's check the gym."

We went to the storage rooms under the gym.

They were locked. But luckily for us, I was on gate duty, so I had a master key that would open any door in school.

"Unh…" Saotome-kun pushed the heavy door open, and went inside.

"It was closed, so she's probably not in here," I said, peeking in. It was dark, so we turned on the lights. There was just one small fluorescent light, though, and it didn't penetrate past the piles of mats, springboards, and other gym equipment.

"But she might be hiding somewhere," Tanaka-kun said, moving to follow Saotome-kun inside.

But Saotome-kun came walking back towards us, waving his hands.

"Nobody here. And definitely no signs of anyone having been here."

***

"—Nothing here," said Saotome Masami. Behind him were the blanket and heater that Echoes had used, and several scattered food wrappers. They were hidden in shadow, and from where they stood at the entrance, Tanaka Shiro and Niitoki Kei weren't able to see them.

"Any cigarette butts?" Kei asked.

Masami made a show of looking behind him, then shook his head.

At his feet was a little bell that Kamikishiro had kept on her school bag.

"Let's try somewhere else."

"Right. Saotome-kun, come on out of there. I'll lock up."

"Mm," Masami said, leaving the evidence where it was, turning out the lights as he left.

"Where should we look next?" Kei asked, locking the door and turning towards the two boys.

"It just occurred to me, but maybe we should use the PA system to summon Kirima Nagi," Masami suggested.

He had confirmed the presence of Echoes, and he knew that Echoes was presumably moving with Kirima Nagi. It was time to move the plan forward to stage two.

***

"The PA system?" I said, blinking at Saotome-kun.

"Yeah. That key can get us in the broadcast room, right?"

"Well, yes, it can…but won't we get in trouble?"

"Probably," Saotome-kun admitted. "But there's no other students around, and the only teacher here is the one on night watch. I'd be more surprised *if* anyone cares enough to yell at us."

"Mmm, well…it *would* be faster. Okay. I'll handle the teacher."

"Thank you for this," Tanaka-kun said apologetically.

"Not like I'm doing it for you," I said. "I'm worried about Naoko-san too." Why was I being so snotty? I was irritating myself. I was only doing this because I couldn't settle down without making things clear. Only my words were impressive.

But I *was* worried about Naoko.

If Kirima Nagi had gotten her mixed up in something, and if it had gone bad, I had to try and stop it…sounding very much like the ardent discipline committee president, aren't I? I never meant to turn into something like that.

"C-come on," I said, agitated, and set off, the two boys following me.

Unfortunately, being at the head of the party didn't do anything for my image. It made me look even more stuck up. Dang.

2.

"Will Kirima Nagi-san, second year, class D, please report to the broadcast office? If you're still in the building, we would like to talk to you regarding Kamikishiro Naoko-san. Repeat, will Kirima Nagi-san, second year, class D …"

Tanaka Shiro's voice echoed through the darkened school.

Of course, it reached the ears of Nakayama Haruo, the one teacher still in the school on night watch duty.

But all he said was, "Umph…" He then slumped onto the table, knocking over his instant ramen, and started snoring.

He was the guardian of the master key that the discipline committee member had, and he was supposed to take it from them and record this in the log, but he was conked out before he could perform his duty.

"Uhn…nah…"

But this was not because of any laziness on his part.

His hands dangled towards the floor, much too limply for normal sleep. His face was pressed against the desk, his neck bent as far as it would go, and he was virtually guaranteed a stiff neck in the morning.

"Uhmph…unh, nahhhhhr…"

His snores were not considered attractive at the best of times, but now they sounded like a stray dog starving to death.

He was not asleep; he had clearly been knocked unconscious.

Nor was he alone in the room.

There was a girl standing next to him.

"………"

She glared up at the speakers as the voice flowed out of them.

There was a sweet, strange smell in the room. The smell had been enough to knock Nakayama Haruo out, but the long, black haired, beautiful girl did not even raise an eyebrow.

Of course not. She was the source of the smell.

Less than ten seconds after the PA announcement began, she was out the door of the night watch room and heading up the stairs.

For many years afterwards, Nakayama Haruo was to suffer a mysterious phenomenon similar to LSD flashbacks (though he was quite certain that he had never tried any drugs) in which his daily routine was abruptly disrupted by illusions similar to intense migraines.

Certainly, this mysterious "disease" was a curse, but he had no idea how insanely lucky he really was.

The only reason he had survived was by the whim of a killer, the fleeting thought that perhaps she had killed too many people already.

***

"——?!" Kirima Nagi heard the announcement as well, and looked up.

She was busy prying open the lockers of every student in the school and searching the contents. Naturally, she was looking for traces of the Manticore. Echoes stood beside her, disguised in a school uniform.

"How do they know I'm still at the school? And what's this about Naoko?"

"Broadcast office…" Echoes plucked the words out of the broadcast, and spoke them.

"Can you sense something, Echoes?!" Kirima Nagi asked. Kamikishiro Naoko had explained to her that he could sense the presence of his clone, the Manticore.

"…………" Echoes put his finger on his forehead and tried to sense it, but shook his head, apparently drawing a blank.

"But an obvious summons like that…why the hell would it need to hide?" Nagi said angrily.

Echoes simply shook his head. He knew only that the Manticore had learned far more about human society than he had managed. This was a trap.

"…………"

He put his hand on Nagi's shoulder, and pushed her backwards. Signaling her not to follow.

"Why not? It's a trap?" Nagi said. She knew it too.

Echoes nodded.

"That's why we have to go," Nagi said quietly. "We don't play into this trap and it'll change its face and make a run for it. It'll leave the school. We'll never catch it then."

"…………"

Echoes watched the fearless girl carefully. In his heart, he whispered.

(Which is it…?)

But the girl who could hear that voice was no more.

Nagi pulled a pair of leather gloves out of her skirt, put them on, and took a stun gun off of the belt that she wore around her waist. The belt and gloves failed to match her uniform at all.

She squeezed the grip once, testing it.

With a crackle, a two million volt firework flew through the air.

***

"She's not coming," Tanaka-kun whispered. It had been at least five minutes since our broadcast.

"The teacher isn't here either. What's going on?" I asked. I was pretty sure Nakayama-sensei was on duty tonight. He was a little neurotic, but he definitely was not the type to let small things go, and an unscheduled broadcast was sure to set him off. Was he asleep?

"…………" Saotome-kun stood deep in thought, frowning.

"What now?" Tanaka-kun asked, turning to look at us, unable to wait.

"One more time," Saotome-kun whispered.

"There's no way she didn't hear that. Maybe she *has* gone home." I spread my hands.

"Yeah," grunted Tanaka-kun.

Saotome-kun said again, more forcefully, "Come on, let's do it again!"

But when he reached for the switch, all the lights in the room suddenly went out.

"—Wah?!"

There were no windows in the broadcast office. It was pitch black.

"A b-blackout?" I said, recovering slightly.

"Damn, the breakers!" snapped Saotome-kun angrily. I wasn't sure what he meant for a second, but of course, if the circuit breakers went, so would the lights. Made perfect sense. He was clearly a fast thinker.

But why would the breakers trip? Unless it was done deliberately, they only tripped when someone was using too much electricity…

Fumbling around in the darkness, I managed to get the door open at last, and moonlight streamed in through the windows in the hall.

There was a black shadow standing right in front of me.

I didn't even have time to look. The shadow pushed something towards me, and a shockwave hit my body.

"Hhh…"

A sound somewhere between a breath and a scream came out of my mouth, and I crumpled to the floor. I couldn't move.

"President?" Saotome-kun cried from behind me. It sounded so far away. The shadow slipped swiftly past me, and launched itself at Saotome-kun.

The impact of him hitting the ground carried through the floorboards to me.

"Wh-who are you?" Tanaka-kun shrieked.

That was the last thing I heard. My consciousness slipped farther and farther away.

***

When I opened my eyes, I found myself tied up and lying on my side on a heavily waxed floor.

It was dark around me. But moonlight came in from somewhere, so it was brighter than the main building had been. Wherever we were was pretty open.

There was only one room in the school this large, with big windows along one side and wooden floors. It was the lecture hall.

(—Wha-what the…?)

I tried to sit up.

But my body was heavy, leaden. It was clear that I still hadn't fully recovered from the impact.

Saotome-kun and Tanaka-kun were lying next to me. I prodded their backs with my knees.

"Hey!"

"Unh," groaned Saotome-kun, stirring, and opening his eyes. "This…" he started to say, but quickly snapped his mouth shut.

"Mm? What?" I asked, looking around. I found what had surprised him. Two figures stood in the direction that he was looking.

"Everyone awake?" said one of them. It was Kirima Nagi.

The other one appeared to be a male student. He was wearing a uniform, but I didn't recognize him.

"What did you do with Kamikishiro-san?" Tanaka-kun asked. It looked like he'd woken up first.

"You're Tanaka Shiro, then? Naoko told me about you," Nagi sighed.

"Kirima-san, what…?" Saotome-kun asked.

Nagi glared at him coldly. "I told you not to get involved, Saotome-kun."

"But what's going on?"

"You don't need to know."

"How can you say that?!" I shouted.

Nagi glared at me, surprised. "Committee President, I know why these two are here, but how did you get mixed up in this?"

"I know Naoko-san too!"

"But don't you think you're trying a little too hard? Caused me no end of confusion."

"I'm the one who's confused!" I shouted, completely forgetting that I was talking to a violence-prone problem child. "Tell me what you think you're doing, right this instant!"

She ignored me, and looked at the boy next to her.

"It's none of them, right, Echoes?"

What did she mean? The boy she'd called Echoes nodded. What a strange nickname.

"None…of them…"

"You'd know, right? Even if it were lying low?"

"Kn-know…"

"None of them have been 'altered.' I see."

Watching the two of them nod at each other pissed me off. "Stop whispering cryptically at each other! And you! You aren't even a student here! I've never seen you before in my life!"

I'm not bragging, but if you're on gate duty often enough, you do end up knowing everyone at school.

Nagi looked at me. "I apologize. We no longer suspect you. Time for you to go on home."

This was much too selfish. "When hell freezes over!" I snapped. Somehow, I managed to get to my feet, despite the ropes binding me. I doubt I could do that twice. It's a stunt you can only pull off when you're too angry to notice.

"Mm?" Nagi frowned.

"I told you to explain yourself! How am I supposed to just forget a thing like this?"

"Well, well, well. I guess we see how you became committee president," Nagi said, glaring at me. She looked like a *yakuza*. "But you need to keep quiet about this."

"Why should I?" I glared back at her.

"For your own good," she said coldly.

"Raaarh!" I snarled, contorting my body in anger. Since my hands and feet were tied, this made me lose my balance, and I fell over again.

(Oops…!)

I was just about to fall flat on my face when I felt somebody catch me.

It was the boy who'd been standing next to Nagi, "Echoes."

I looked up at him. He nodded, and undid my bonds.

From this close, he had a rather gentle face.

"Th-thanks…" I said, rubbing the rope burns.

He proceeded to undo Tanaka-kun and Saotome-kun as well. We were tied pretty tightly, but he pulled the ropes off like he was playing cat's cradle. He looked frail, but he must have been pretty strong.

For some reason, he reminded me of Christopher Lambert's Tarzan. His hair wasn't as long, but he gave off a similar air. Kind of unworldly.

"Kirima-san, who is this guy?" Saotome-kun asked. Feeling a little jealous, I guess.

"Mm…uh…well…my boyfriend," Nagi replied, clearly lying.

"You can't fool me that easily. What are you doing here? Where's Naoko-san?" I glared at Nagi again.

"R-right! What did you do to Kamikishiro-san?!" Tanaka-kun yelled, turning on Nagi the moment he was free.

"I'm worried about Naoko myself," Nagi said painfully, not meeting his gaze. She clearly knew something.

"Tell us. We can help."

"No, you can't," Nagi snapped.

"Why not?!"

"This is not a normal situation. Unless you're screwed up like me, you can't possibly tackle it."

She didn't hesitate at all to call herself screwed up.

I shrank back a little at the strength of her words.

Saotome-kun spoke up, "Normal still not good enough, hunh?" It was clear that he was quite bitter about something.

He smiled a little. I looked at his face, and for some reason, felt the hairs on my neck stand up.

It was just an ordinary, affable smile, but there was something unnaturally relaxed about it, like when you're playing a video game for the thousandth time, and a pattern you're particularly good at shows up. His smile was calm and ruthless.

"Mm…" Nagi frowned. She must have said the same thing when she rejected him.

"Is Kamikishiro-san okay?!" Tanaka-kun insisted.

Nagi said bluntly, bitterly, "Shiro-kun, right? You should forget about her."

"What do you mean?!"

"…………"

Nagi said nothing else.

3.

Nagi and this Echoes guy led us out of the lecture hall. "Go straight home," Nagi insisted.

"I have to give the key back," I said sullenly. I wasn't finished sulking about not getting an explanation. "Maybe I'll report you."

"Whatever," Nagi said airily.

"What's wrong with you?" I retorted. "What makes you think you have to be personally responsible for everything? Can't you just let things be?!"

"Now, now, Committee President," Saotome-kun said, patting me on the shoulders.

"But—!" I insisted.

But Saotome-kun was completely calm, the exact opposite of my state of mind. He spoke to me like he was soothing a fretful baby. "There's nothing you can do. Kirima-san has things she needs to do." It was like he knew what those things were.

"…………"

He was definitely too relaxed.

When I held my tongue, he turned back towards Nagi.

At his steady gaze, Nagi awkwardly looked away.

He spoke to her anyway. "Kirima-san. I do understand." He took a mechanical pencil out of his pocket, and spun it around his fingers, very casually.

"We can never be satisfied with 'normal.'"

"......?" Nagi stared at Saotome-kun, baffled. "What?"

"Looking back, I'm glad you rejected me. If I had been with you, then *when I met her, I would've been her enemy.*" He sighed, almost happily.

Nagi frowned. "When you met who? What are you talking about?" She seemed confused. It looked like something about his turn of phrase that bothered her.

A little smile crept up the edges of Saotome-kun's lips. "In other words, I can't help but put you on the side of 'normal,' now." His shoulders slumped.

Then he moved like lightening.

Before I even realized that he'd turned around, his arm was reaching out towards Echoes, who stood behind him.

The mechanical pencil was in his hand. His aim was true. The tip of it stabbed deep into Echoes' throat.

"——?!"

Echoes staggered backwards.

In an instant, Saotome Masami had buried the pencil all the way inside Echoes' throat. Then he turned his attention back towards Nagi.

"Now, you are our enemy."

A shadow fell towards us from above.

We all looked up, and saw a person dropping down from the school roof.

Someone I knew.

Yurihara Minako.

She was looking right at Echoes.

Falling on him…no, attacking him.

"____!"

Blood gushing from his throat, Yurihara Minako cut him open from his shoulder to his waist…with her mere fingers—her nails hideously long.

She'd fallen more than ten meters, but bounded upwards again like a grasshopper.

By God, she wasn't human!

"Ah…" I could do nothing but stand there with my mouth hanging open.

"M-Manticore!" Nagi shrieked, following the leaping monster that looked like Yurihara Minako with her eyes.

That cost her her life.

Saotome Masami was standing right in front of her.

She looked down just in time to see his hand slash downwards.

The knife in his hand flashed.

"____!" Nagi's voice never made it to words. It was a tiny little survival knife, the size of his palm, like a toy, but the blade was sharp, and it sliced her throat open.

"*I just changed teams—from the killed, to the killers.*"

I doubt anyone but Saotome Masami himself could understand the meaning behind his words.

Kirima Nagi spun around, blood spraying from her throat. She fell over.

"____!"

His throat pierced, his torso cut in two, Echoes was still watching Nagi. He clearly wasn't human either.

He dodged Yurihara Minako as she attacked again, and dashed to Nagi's side.

Ignoring Saotome Masami, who backed away, Echoes scooped up Nagi's convulsing body, and leapt away. He cleared the roof of the school in a single jump, vanishing into the night sky.

He ran away…?

"Chase him! This is your chance!" Saotome Masami shouted, and Yurihara Minako reversed her course, leaping back the way she had come.

I was dumbfounded.

Beside me, Tanaka-kun wailed, then ran away screaming.

Saotome Masami swung towards me.

I was frozen stiff, and I couldn't move a muscle.

"Heh heh heh," he laughed. His smile was exactly the same as it had been a moment before, back when he was on our side.

But this boy had just killed another human being…

My knees rattled. I was shaking with fear.

"To be honest, the plan was for Kirima Nagi to kill me here, but oh well. This way was pretty fun too," he said, grinning. Like everything was normal.

"I could get addicted to doing things myself," he commented, walking towards me, moonlight glittering off the knife in his hand.

***

As Echoes fled upwards to the roof, he realized that there was little power left in his body.

The pencil from a moment before—instead of lead, it had been filled with a fatal poison created by the Manticore. He was infected.

"……!"

He quickly pulled the pencil out of his throat. But it was too late.

His feet and hands felt numb. Injuries that his massive regenerative powers should have healed instantly showed no signs of improving.

But what had happened?

That boy was the Manticore's ally?

He hadn't been brainwashed. Echoes was sure of that. But why would a normal human be working with a monster?

Echoes glanced down at Nagi.

She was no longer breathing. Her pupils were dilated, nothing reflected in her eyes. Her lips were half open, a stream of blood flowing out of them. She wasn't moving.

This girl had protected everyone from the shadows, in secret, and it had killed her.

"…………"

Echoes stared down at her ashen face.

(Which is it…?)

He wondered inside. But only Kamikishiro Naoko could answer, and sadly, she was gone.

Yurihara Minako hit the roof behind him, giving chase.

Echoes gathered Nagi up again, and leapt off of the roof.

"You can't get away from me!" The Manticore yelled, following him.

She was smiling. Saotome Masami's plan was going perfectly.

Echoes was running, but he was too badly wounded. He could not hope to hide.

She was an imperfect copy, and would never have been his equal in a fair fight, but now the tables were turned.

When she next caught sight of Echoes, he was abandoning Kirima Nagi's body in the bushes of the school's garden. Clearly, he was trying to lighten the load, but it was too late.

Grinning from ear to ear, the Manticore flung herself at the slow-moving Echoes.

Her kick sent Echoes flying.

***

There was a low thud from the school garden.

I snapped out of it.

Saotome Masami was right in front of me, waving a knife.

I narrowly dodged it by rolling on the ground.

I got my feet up from under me and tried to run, but my right foot slipped, and I fell again.

I looked down.

My hands were resting in a pool of Kirima Nagi's blood.

"Aaaaahhhh!" and at last, I was able to scream.

Saotome Masami came after me.

I tried to spin around. My fingers touched something.

It gleamed. It was the stun gun that Kirima Nagi had dropped.

"……!"

I snatched up the weapon.

"Grr…" Saotome Masami scowled.

"St-stay back!" I pointed the weapon in his direction, and squeezed the switch-like thing on the side.

With a crackle, fireworks spat off of the tip, but they were only a few centimeters long. It was but a tiny little light, and it didn't look at all threatening.

"Hmph," Saotome Masami smiled, coldly. "What are you going to do to me with *that*? That kind of weapon can't kill anyone."

"Wh-what are you people? That—Yurihara Minako *thing*...what is it?!"

"She is Yurihara Minako, but she is not Yurihara Minako. The original is dead. She is the Manticore."

"Manticore...?" I could swear I'd heard that name somewhere. In a computer game or something. I'm sure it meant...

...Man-eater.

Oh. God. That meant...that meant Naoko-san was...

Saotome Masami saw my expression, and guessed what I was thinking. He grinned. "*Exactly. She's already been digested.*"

He said it so normally. Without a shred of guilt.

"A-and all the other people who vanished?"

"Mostly. Well, there may be a few girls who just ran away on their own."

"And Kirima Nagi was looking for you..."

That's why she captured us. But she thought we had nothing to do with it, so she released us, without realizing that one of her enemies was hiding among us...

"You used us as cover, didn't you?"

"You had your uses. She was a fool. She allied herself with Echoes, but it never occurred to her that his enemy might have allies as well."

His complete composure put a match to the flames of

anger inside me. They soon banished my fear.

"So you lied when you said you loved her?"

"No, that was the truth. *But I no longer need her.* Still, I wasn't going to let the Manticore have her; no, I wanted to kill her with my own hands. Do you know how good that feels?"

"How the hell would I know *that*?"

I thrust my weapon towards him. He dodged easily.

"Beautiful, President. I love your eyes. I love strong-willed, powerful eyes."

Grrr. "You little…" I swung my weapon wildly, not getting anywhere near him.

Then something passed over my head.

It was "Echoes." He slammed into the ground. He'd been thrown there.

He was torn to pieces.

While I was distracted, Saotome Masami kicked my hand.

"Ah?!" I yelped, but the stun gun was already flung out of my reach.

From behind me, Yurihara Minako yelled, "Enough, Saotome-kun! I'll finish things."

"Okay," Saotome Masami replied, picking up the stun gun and stepping away. I ran over to Echoes.

He was a wreck. His right arm was half torn off his shoulder, and there were holes all over his body. He was covered in blood.

"E-Echoes?" I said, pulling him upright.

He opened his eyes feebly.

A pained moan escaped his purple lips.

"President, it's no use asking him to save you. He's almost dead," Yurihara Minako—the Manticore—said, laughing.

"That wasn't so hard. You might even have been able to

win without any tricks," Saotome Masami said, evidently enjoying himself.

"I never thought he would be this weak," the Manticore replied, amused. "I'm sure he used to be stronger."

I glared at her.

"You aren't human! You're both devils!"

***

As he lay dying, Echoes heard the girl holding him shout, "You aren't human!"

Not human. She meant they weren't fit to be called human. He still didn't understand.

Which were humans?

Humans had captured him for being different, and forcefully and quite mercilessly studied his body. Humans had made the Manticore. But the people who had saved him, the cloaked boy in the black hat, Kamikishiro Naoko, and Kirima Nagi, were all human too.

Which is it?

Which is the truth?

"Ha ha ha! You are stupid, aren't you?!" The Manticore laughed, mocking the girl. "I never was human! And Saotome-kun is nothing like you foolish humans. Devils? Fine with me! I think I like being called a devil!"

"You will be destroyed!" The girl shouted back, not at all cowed. "I will die here, and so will this man, but there will be other people who will stand in your way! No matter where you hide, there will be people who can't ignore the distortions in the world that you're trying to create! And you will be found again, just like Kirima Nagi found you!" Big tears were running down her cheeks.

She was sad.

Because she was about to die?

Then why was she holding him so tightly?

It was as if she was protecting him from the Manticore.

Like Kamikishiro Naoko had, when she found him wounded in town.

(Humans…)

He had no more time.

He had to make a choice.

***

"Like Kirima Nagi?" the Manticore chuckled. "I think I'll be *her* next."

"……?" I didn't know what she meant. I had to ask. "What do you mean?"

"Just that I'll change from Yurihara Minako into Kirima Nagi."

At first, I couldn't comprehend this. My mind went blank. Then I was horrified. "W-what?!"

"She's an ideal specimen. She's crazy, so nobody will say anything if I behave a little oddly; she's rich, and has a vast information network set up. It's perfect. There will be a commotion when Yurihara Minako vanishes, which I would prefer to avoid, but the benefits far outweigh *that*."

"……!" I shuddered, turning to look at Saotome Masami. He had said that he *no longer needed her*. Because *he had a new girlfriend now*.

Saotome Masami stared back at me, expressionless.

I had no words.

"As for you, Niitoki Kei," the Manticore continued. "The world will never know you've died. We will alter you, and make a slave of you. You'll be moving around, but you will have no heart. Even if you meet a boy you liked, you will feel nothing."

I was horrified again.

I could see it.

The Manticore disguised as Nagi, and me standing beside her as her slave...I could see myself on gate duty, Nagi beside me, and I'm pointing her to her next meal...even if the boy I had once loved and his pretty girlfriend came, I would think nothing, simply greet them mechanically...

And that's not all. The Manticore's terrifying words gave me a glimpse of a higher purpose.

She and Saotome Masami weren't killing for their own self-preservation. This was just one part of their plan to take control of the world from us humans.

But if they graduated, and went out of school, what would happen to the world?

She came closer to me.

"......!"

I hugged Echoes' body tightly.

Then...

Echoes slowly raised his wounded arm.

It was shaking. His fist wasn't clenched or open, his fingers just hung there limply.

He pointed his hand at the Manticore.

"What? What's that mean? You still think you can do something to stop me?" The Manticore smirked.

"............" But Echoes wasn't looking at her.

He was looking at the stars in the sky behind her.

And he suddenly spoke, using actual words, not to anybody, but to the *sky* above.

"My body into information, transmit to source!"

And the air around me was filled with white light.

4.

That evening, a strange electrical disturbance was recorded in the area. Satellite broadcast monitors all went white, computer hard drives were cleared of all data, and a multitude of other similar unnatural phenomenon were encountered. The television stations and newspaper offices were deluged with questions and complaints. There were several investigations launched, with no real satisfactory results. But a number of witnesses said, "About that time, I could swear I saw the sky glow. It was just for a second, but it was like a bright light was launched from the ground into the sky." But these reports were never connected to anything, and were eventually buried and forgotten.

***

…I know what I saw.

Echoes changed into light, and that light swallowed the Manticore.

And a second before it did, Saotome Masami leapt in front of the Manticore, shielding her with his body—

I don't know what he was thinking, why he was on the side of the Manticore, and frankly, I don't want to know.

But there was one thing that I did have to admit...he might have killed a number of people for the Manticore, but that casual disregard for life sure included his own.

Saotome Masami was swept up in the torrent of light, his body blown away, not a trace of it left.

He was disintegrated...no, he was erased.

But moments before Echoes had self-destructed, the Manticore had been flung aside by her companion and out of the beam's path.

"......!"

Even as I was flung aside by the shockwave, I desperately struggled to grasp the situation.

But no, I didn't understand *anything*.

From my point of view, there was absolutely no way for me to grasp the first thing about what had just happened.

What the hell was Echoes? How could something that looked like a human turn into light and explode?! And what 'information' was he 'transmitting'? To who? I simply had no way of knowing.

(What's happening—?!)

I hit the ground and rolled, screaming with frustration inside.

When I finally managed to stop myself, there was no light left around me.

Grunting in pain, I sat up, looked in front of me, and gasped.

She was standing there alone.

Half of her body was burned black, and smoke was rising off of it. The uniform she'd been wearing had been blown away, and beneath the moonlight, every inch of her slim, limber body was exposed.

"…………"

She was gazing blankly at the sky.

She didn't seem to be looking at anything.

"…………"

Her lips trembled. Like they were scrambling to form words that never emerged.

"Ah…ahh…"

There was no expression on her face. It had been replaced by emptiness.

The face of someone that had lost something that they valued more than their own life.

As if half of her body had been torn away.

As if her capacity for joy had been pulled up by the roots.

She looked as if she could no longer perceive any meaning, like there was nothing left for her.

"Aaaaaarrrrrggggghhhhhhhhh!!"

Somewhere, her endless scream turned into a howl.

It was the sound of her heart breaking.

The scream seemed to shake the moon.

"…………"

I sat and watched, nailed to the spot.

But then I realized that was the last thing I should be doing.

(G-got to run…!)

As I tried to get to my feet, the gravel scrunched beneath me.

Like a mechanical response, the Manticore's battered face

swung towards me.

Our eyes met.

A shiver ran down my spine.

Even by the light of the moon, I could tell her eyes were blood red. The whites were completely soaked in crimson hostility.

"You die…!" she howled. "I'll kill every last one of you!!"

As if her voice had been a trigger, I shot to my feet, and ran for it.

Naturally, she came after me.

I was running, but from the sound of it, she was walking, dragging one leg.

But the sound was getting closer.

(Waaaah!)

At the time, I was convinced that fear had finally driven me round the bend.

I was hearing things.

I could hear a melody coming through the bushes in front of me—an impossible, unnatural melody.

Someone was whistling.

Whistling a tune that should never be whistled, Wagner's "Die Meistersinger von Nurnberg."

Unnatural or not, at that moment I had no other straws to grasp at.

I ran for my life towards the sound.

When I was almost there, my leg slipped.

"Aah—!" I screamed, pitching forward, falling flat on my face. I smacked my forehead on the ground, and everything went black for a moment.

The whistling stopped.

I could hear the sound of the Manticore's footsteps, several times louder than it had been a moment before.

"____!"

I spun around, and the Manticore's hand was already reaching towards me.

This is it. I'm going to die…!

Just as that thought crossed my mind…

Fwsh!

It was the sound of something cutting through the air.

And then…the Manticore's hand flew off, with a grotesque slicing sound…

It had been severed from her body and was now spinning through the air!

(Wha…?)

I saw something flash.

Like string.

It twisted like it was alive, and wrapped around the Manticore's neck.

It tightened.

"____?!"

The Manticore's expression changed. She snatched at her throat with both hands. But she only had one, and the fingers of it tried to get a grip on the string wrapped around her throat.

It wasn't a string. It was a horrifically thin metal wire.

'Ah,' I thought. I had my answer. The reason I had suddenly tripped and fallen was because this wire had been strung across my path.

One end of the wire appeared to be tied around a tree.

The other end led into the shadow of the school building.

When I looked in that direction, I felt my brains pour out of my ears.

"It can't be—?!" I shouted.

There was a figure there, leaning backwards, pulling on the wire with black gloves. It wore a cape and a black hat shaped like a pipe. It was the very creature that all the girls in my class had been gossiping about.

"...The wrist was charred enough for me to cut through, but the neck seems to be stronger," it said.

The androgynous voice, neither male nor female, was exactly as the rumors said.

But the face...was...

"M-M-Miyashita-san?!"

Yes, it was clearly that of my classmate, Miyashita Touka.

"Currently, I am Boogiepop," she...no, he said clearly, in a boy's voice.

"Gh...?!" gurgled the Manticore, eyes widening in surprise.

She was no more able to take this in than I was.

The wire was sunk deep into the skin of her throat. She was struggling to loosen it with her fingers, but it was cutting the fingers instead, and they were bleeding.

"Ghh...ghhhh...!

"You call yourself the Manticore?" Boogiepop said quietly. "You are much stronger than a human, but I can make free use of the strength that humans unconsciously keep in reserve to avoid exceeding the limits of their flesh. *Since I am only borrowing this body*."

Then he suddenly shouted, "Now, Shiro-kun! Shoot it!"

I had no time to ponder what he meant. No sooner had the words left his mouth than an arrow pierced the Manticore's chest.

I knew that arrow.

It was a duralumin arrow, that kind that the archery team used.

I spun around, and behind me was Tanaka-kun, who had not run away after all, but holding a sturdy glass fiber bow, aimed at me—no, at the Manticore.

Her head was trapped. She couldn't dodge.

"Agh…"

I wonder what the Manticore thought at that moment, when she knew that she had lost.

She didn't look at the arrow in her chest, or at Boogiepop, or at the archer.

I saw an expression steal over that empty face. To me, it looked like…relief.

"Shoot her head!" Boogiepop said, showing no mercy.

He killed her when she was at her most beautiful, before she had a chance to grow ugly; killed her without pain…just as the stories said.

Tanaka-kun let go.

The arrow was flung off the bowstring, and hit Yurihara Minako's face dead center, smashing her head.

For an instant, what looked like cracks ran all down her body, and then she crumbled, changing into a purple smoke.

The smoke drifted in all directions, carried away on the wind.

A little of it drifted past my nose. It smelt of horribly thick, fresh blood.

***

"............"

I couldn't stand up.

Tanaka-kun came running over.

"A-are you okay?"

"Um…y-yeah…" I shook my head, trying to recover some clarity.

But Miyashita-san walked in front of me again in that Boogiepop costume, and my thoughts scattered again.

"Wh-what is that?!" I asked Tanaka-kun, clinging to him like a toddler.

He shook his head. "I don't know. He stopped me on my way back from practice, offered to help…you know him?"

"I…kind of know…of him…"

Boogiepop undid the wire from around the tree, and headed to the bushes where Kirima Nagi lay.

"The Manticore said Echoes was surprisingly weak. I wonder why…" he muttered. He (or was it a she after all?) kicked Kirima Nagi.

Nagi had been killed, her throat sliced open…but her body shook, and she sat up.

She'd come back to life.

"He gave you part of his life. You've escaped death again."

Tanaka-kun and I could do nothing but gape.

Nagi moaned and clutched her forehead. She'd lost a lot of blood, and must be anemic.

"Hello, Fire Witch," Boogiepop said.

"You again," Nagi replied, not at all surprised. She sighed. "If you were out, why didn't you come sooner?"

"Your actions finally allowed me to uncover the nature of the danger."

"I gotta be me all the damn time, but you only bother coming out when the shit hits the fan. You selfish bastard."

"Don't say that," he replied. It sounded like they'd known each other for years.

"Is…is it over?"

"Yes. Thanks to Echoes' sacrifice and the committee president's courage."

"I see…" Nagi tried to stand, but wavered and fell over again.

Boogiepop made no effort to help her, instead coming back in our direction.

"I leave her in your hands. I'll take care of the clean up," he told us.

"…………" We made no response.

Boogiepop picked up the Manticore's hand from the ground. He looked up at me, and made a strange expression, narrowing one eye, like he was smiling, but not quite. It was like he was playing dumb.

"Niitoki Kei—you certainly do have a strong will. It's because of people like you that the world manages to remain a halfway decent place. In the world's stead, I thank you."

It was like a speech from a play. I had no idea what it meant.

Leaving me standing there stunned, he fled like the wind, turning the corner behind the gym and vanishing from sight.

And that was how it ended.

5.

"But how did Boogiepop become a rumor? He's supposed to be a mysterious figure, his identity a secret. Who started all the legends about him?" I asked Kirima Nagi the next day after class.

"Probably Miyashita Touka herself," Nagi answered. We were alone in the room. Everyone else had already left.

"Eh? What do you mean?"

"Miyashita Touka is unaware that she has an alter-ego known as Boogiepop inside of her. But she knows it unconsciously. You know, like how you talk about yourself, but say it's a friend of yours? Same principle, she just told other people about her other self."

"That's it?"

"You should probably ask Suema about it. Well, not specifically, but she can explain it way better than I can."

"Hmm…I don't really get it."

"I don't know much about that bastard myself," she sighed. "Did everyone make a fuss when Yurihara Minako didn't show?"

"The teacher asked if any of us knew anything, but nobody answered. It's too soon for anyone to realize she's actually missing, so not much is going on yet. But for a straight 'A' student like her, skipping's enough to get the gossip going."

"Hunh…"

I'd called Yurihara-san's house the day before, but the answering machine lead me to believe that both her parents were off on business trips. Nobody knew she hadn't come home. It looked as though the Manticore had deliberately chosen to make her move while they were out of town.

But all hell would break loose in a day or two. Yurihara Minako would cause a lot more problems for the school than any of the other girls had.

Saotome Masami would be buried under her shadow. His parents probably already knew he hadn't come home, but he was a boy, so they were unlikely to worry all that much if he was out all night.

"When was the real Yurihara…when was she replaced?"

"Not sure. But a pretty long time ago. She always had been missing. It was just that up until now, we simply hadn't noticed she was gone."

"I guess that's true…"

We both hung our heads.

It was a strange feeling.

We couldn't tell anyone the truth. If we did, it would just make things worse for all of us. And even then, if word about Echoes got out to the institution that made the Manticore, it would just be asking for trouble.

"So, all it ultimately amounts to is nothing?"

"It's better that way."

"Yeah…"

We stood up.

Most of the other students had gone home, and the sports teams and clubs were all in full session. There was nobody roaming the halls or stopped at the shoe lockers.

We headed for the gates, and the girl on gate duty was very happy to see me.

"Ah! President! Thank god you're here! Could you take over for me for a minute? I really gotta pee!"

I smiled and nodded, and she bolted off into the school.

"Everyone likes you," Nagi grinned.

"Or likes using me," I grimaced. I remembered all the times that Kamikishiro Naoko had talked me into fudging the numbers to make her on time. Which is how we got to be friends in the first place.

"Naoko-san is really…?" I said softly, suddenly horribly sad.

"Yeah…I think so," Nagi whispered sorrowfully.

When Tanaka-kun had left us the day before, he'd said, "I don't know how to say this, but I feel like I should thank you all for Kamikishiro-san. Thank you."

He was almost crying.

"Tanaka-kun, what did you really think of Naoko-san?" I'd asked.

He looked at me sadly. "Truthfully, if we had found her, I would've told her that I wanted to break up. But now…I'm not so sure."

"Hmmm…" was all I said.

I couldn't figure out what I should say to her other lover, Kimura Akio. We would probably never speak to each other. If someday someone were to tell him, that would be—

But we all had to return to our daily routine, just exactly as things had been before.

"Naoko said something strange once," Nagi said, looking up at the sky.

"She said Echoes was an angel. That the lord of the heavens had ordered him to investigate, and make the final decision on whether mankind should be allowed to live, or if it should be destroyed. He came here to find out if humans were a benevolent existence, or a malevolent one. If we were the latter, he would end our history."

I was taken aback. "An angel?"

"I mean, I'm pretty sure she was reading a lot into this. She had a tendency to blow everything out of proportion. My guess is Echoes and Manticore were both failed experiments in biotechnology. But if she was right…"

"……"

"We're still here. Looks like we're off the hook this time," she smiled sadly.

She had to say that. She couldn't let her friend's death be in vain.

But I couldn't smile.

Nagi hadn't seen the end of Echoes.

But I had. Clearly.

That light had made it as if Saotome Masami had never existed in the first place. It had turned the nearly immortal Manticore into a burnt crisp.

That was no biotechnological experiment.

It had beamed itself into space, but if something like that were fired at the earth over and over again…

"Then the one who really saved the world…"

"Wasn't me, wasn't Boogiepop…ultimately, it was that

lonely little love-struck girl who was nice to Echoes. And we can't even thank her for it now," Nagi sounded almost irritated.

"…………"

I had no answer for her. I just stared silently at the sky. It seemed so far away.

**

As Nagi and I stood there staring absently into the clear blue sky, a boy and a girl came walking together towards us. When I saw them, I couldn't stop myself from exclaiming, "Ah!"

One of them was Miyashita Touka. The other one was a third year student with a promising career in design that I had fallen for and had my heart broken by, Takeda Keiji-sempai.

He looked a little nervous when he saw me, so I spoke to him first, to show him that he needn't worry about it. "Oh, *sempai*," I said as cheerfully as I could manage.

"Hey," he said vaguely.

Suddenly, Nagi was standing in front of Miyashita-san. "Hmm. So you're Miyashita Touka," she said. It seemed that this was her first time meeting this side of her.

"Y-yes…" Miyashita-san said, nodding, in a cute little voice as far removed from Boogiepop's boyish tones as possible.

"I'm Kirima. Nice to meet you," Nagi said, and held out her hand.

To an outsider, it must have looked like the school delinquent was out to get her.

"Hey!" Takeda-sempai said, stepping up to protect her.

But Miyashita-san shook her head. "You too," she said, shaking Nagi's hand. Perhaps she understood this unconsciously as well.

"See ya," Nagi said, giving her a wry grin.

The two of them went through the gates, and I let out a big sigh, and stared up at the sky again.

I wasn't able to look Miyashita-san in the eye. I tried to smile at her, but I just couldn't.

There are too many things that just aren't clear.

It should be simple to smile at someone, but sometimes that's a terribly difficult and painful thing to do.

"It's so hard to smile…"

"Hm? What do you mean?"

I shook my head. "Never mind. It was nothing."

Nagi looked at me dubiously, but eventually, she looked back up at the sky, and began to whistle.

It was a song I knew. I sang along, softly.

> *"Life is brief, young maiden, fall in love;*
> *before the crimson bloom fades from your lips,*
> *before the tides of passion cool within your hips,*
> *for those of you who know no tomorrow."*

The autumn sky was so bright that it made my eyes water. 'It'll be winter soon,' I thought.

"Boogiepop and Others" closed.

Afterword:
The School in Boogiepop

These days, I rarely have them, but back in my early twenties, I often had dreams about high school. Dreams in which I was going to high school, not dreams about having gone. I'm talking about in the present tense, as a twenty something adult, putting on a uniform (the old kind with the clasp) and going to school. In the dreams, I knew clearly that I had graduated several years before, but I was pretending not to know and going anyway. Since it was a dream, this pretense was enough to fool my classmates. Not one of them ever noticed that I had no business being at school. Neither did the teachers. I sat in the corner of my class, in the dreams, thinking about how much I really shouldn't be there.

The school in the dreams was not the Kanagawa Prefectural Noba High School that I had actually gone to. Rather, it was a school I had never seen. (For starters, Noba uniforms didn't have a clasp; they were blazers.) Nevertheless, I knew all kinds of things about that school. To make a long story short, the setting for *Boogiepop and Others*, Shinyo Academy, is that school from my dreams, the only part of this novel that is fantasy. The rest is something different.

I think I failed miserably at being a teenage boy. I never once thought I was young, or had a future. (I often do now.) I never actively participated in class or anything else. I just sat there, wondering what I was doing there, and after I graduated, I wondered why I had spent so much time thinking about those sorts of things. I don't particularly understand myself.

So, even now, I don't really get the idea of going to school. I was twenty-eight when I wrote this novel, and over ten years have passed since I graduated. Even if I try to find the answer, I no longer have a school to go to, so the whole thing is permanently out of reach. It's all too late now. It's one of many, but this "what did I do in school?" question is a pretty big trauma for me. It's like my first love that I never asked out. Augh! I was a dirty little angst-ridden idiot without a single thought for love. I imagine the reason behind the dreams is my conviction that I would be much better at being a high school student now.

Ultimately, school is a place where you have to be with others. That's all. It ends without you ever really under-standing much about each other, but even so, you bump into a lot of people and a lot of thoughts, and you still come back for more. Sadly, schools are not exactly set up to preserve that diversity. (Right, my readers in school?) I can't help but think that's a crying shame, but the entire world seems to work that way, and school isn't that unique of a place in the world. That's why, in my dreams, I'm always thinking, "God, I really hated that guy, but now I wish I'd known him a little better." And I do all this while sitting there in the corner of the room.

(This is less of an afterword than a confession, isn't it?)
(Ah, whatever.)

BGM "HEARTBREAKER" (live ver.) by Grand Funk Railroad.

ROLL CALL
at Shinyo Academy

CLASS ROSTER
Who's Who

First Year, Class D

Kusatsu Akiko (F)
Noguchi Sachiko (F)
Saotome Masami (M)
Tanaka Shiro (M)

First Year, Class F

Sakamoto Jun (M)

Second Year, Class B

Kimura Akio (M)

Second Year, Class C

Miyashita Touka / Boogiepop (F)

Second year, Class D

Kirima Nagi (F)
Kinoshita Kyoko (F)
Saito Rie (F)
Suema Kazuko (F)
Watanabe Misaki (F)
Yurihara Minako/Manticore (F)

Second Year, Class F

Niitoki Kei (F)
Suzumiya Takako (F)

Third Year, Class F

Kamikishiro Naoko (F)
Sasaki (F)
Takeda Keiji (M)

Teacher

Nakayama Haruo (M)

(F) = female   (M) = male   (O) = other

COUPLES
Who's Shacking Up With Whom

Kimura Akio (M)
Kamikishiro Naoko (F)
Tanaka Shiro (M)

Saotome Masami (M)
Yurihara Minako (F) / Manticore (O)

Takeda Keiji (M)
Miyashita Touka (F)

Noguchi Sachiko (F)
Sakamoto Jun (M)

DISCIPLINE COMMITTEE
The Teachers' Pets

Niitoki Kei (F)
Saotome Masami (M)
Tanaka Shiro (M)
Takeda Keiji (M)

THE "IN" CROWD
Movers and Shakers in the Boogiepop Universe

Miyashita Touka (F) / Boogiepop (O)
Yurihara Minako (F) / Manticore (O)
Echoes (M)
Kirima Nagi (F)
Saotome Masami (M)

TRANSLATION NOTES

Translating a foreign language work is a challenging task that can result in a lot of sleepless nights and headaches for the production team involved. The general rule of thumb for any English-language release is to make sure that it retains the intricacies of the source material, while not reading like a literal translation. It's a difficult line to walk, but we at Seven Seas believe that preserving cultural nuance is of utmost importance.

For this reason, we've strived to present a translation that is as close to the original as possible, while keeping the flow of the novel intact. The following pages of translation notes are presented here as a way to offer some additional insight into many of the terms, characters and other cultural items that you may not have understood while reading the novel. These notes also offer a further look into some of the choices that the editorial staff at Seven Seas had to make while bringing the work to you. Enjoy!

COVER

Dual Titles – Though this novel is entitled *Boogiepop and Others*, the *Boogiepop* series is one that is known for carrying multiple titles on many of its covers, and this book is no exception. If you look back at the cover, you'll notice that the title is presented in both English and Japanese. The Japanese title for this novel is a mixture of the Japanese phonetic alphabets, Hirigana and Katakana, as well as a solitary Kanji character, and the title is commonly romanized as "Boogiepop wa Warawanai." However, this Japanese title doesn't translate as "Boogiepop and Others." The title literally translates to either "Boogiepop Doesn't Laugh" or "Boogiepop Doesn't Smile." In essence, this means that the full title for this first novel could be thought of as "Boogiepop wa Warawanai: Boogiepop and Others" or "Boogiepop Doesn't Laugh: Boogiepop and Others"—where the second portion of the title is meant as a subtitle to the work.

Seven Seas has chosen to use the English subtitle of *Boogiepop and Others* as the primary title for this novel to keep it consistent with The Right Stuf International's dvd release of the live action movie, which is itself based upon this novel. Furthermore, we are using *Boogiepop Doesn't Laugh* as the title for the two-volume manga adaptation of this novel—an adaptation written by Kouhei Kadono and illustrated by Kouji Ogata that sheds additional light on events presented in this novel and reveals new events and scenes. We have chosen to split the titles to avoid confusion between the two releases.

INTRODUCTION

Shoji – In Japanese homes, sliding doors that consist of translucent white rice paper stretched over a wooden frame. (pg.19)

Tatami – Traditional straw matting that is commonly used to cover floors. (pg.19)

Three Year Term – As many anime and manga fans are well aware, Japanese high schools tend to focus on three-year terms known as first year, second year and third year, whereas most North American high schools tend to have four-year terms, consisting of ninth through twelfth grades. For clarity's sake, this novel has mostly used first, second and third years, but we have employed the term "senior" in a few spots, referring to a third year student, where it felt more natural from a storytelling standpoint.

Student Discipline Committee – Kei is the president of the discipline committee, and other characters tend to address her as "President." This particular type of committee seems to be a common feature in Japanese high schools, but no one seems to be sure why, since they don't actually do anything. For this reason, this committee should not be confused with the student council, nor should Kei's position be confused with class president.

<u>CHAPTER 1-1</u>

Touka's Name – We have decided not to use the Boogiepop movie and art book's method of romanizing "Miyashita Toka," as the word "*toka*" is a Japanese preposition, and it seems awkward as a name. We've elected to spell her name so that it's similar to the original Japanese pronunciation by retaining the 'tou' sound (pronounced *tô*.)

A Male in a Female's Body – The character of Boogiepop is usually referred to by using male pronouns, but occasionally other characters will claim they aren't really certain if it is a male or female—just that he/she has the same pretty face as Miyashita Touka's. This kind of gender confusion has been a common convention in Japanese literature throughout history.

Sempai and Kouhai – Seven Seas requested that Andrew, the translator, made sure to preserve the terms *sempai* and *kouhai* as much as possible. There are a few exceptions, though. When *sempai* is used in place of "you," we did remove it, as the resulting line would seem too unnatural.

Double Dating – It's pretty unusual for a school to ban dating these days, but Shinyo Academy is unusually strict. The term that Keiji uses in Japanese is "*group kousai*." (pg.26)

Ghost Stories – Once Boogiepop appears in front of the crowd, Keiji compares Boogiepop's face to that of a *nopperabou*—a faceless ghost. This term actually comes from a ghost story that goes something like this: you meet a ghost with no face (a nopperabou), and it frightens you so much that you run down the hill and into the first soba shop you see. As you slurp your noodles, you tell the shop owner about your experience, and he asks, "Did it look...like *this*?" and suddenly, he, too, has no face. (pg.29)

CHAPTER 1-2

Campus Advanced Information Administration System – Originally "Koudo Jouhou Kanri Gakuen System." (pg.32)

Naoko's Song – A very traditional Japanese song that is famous for being in Akira Kurosawa's film *Ikiru*. Rather than use the translation that appears on the Criterion Collection DVD, we've elected to further refine it into verse with a slight rhyme. The original appears as follows:

> *"Inochi mijikashi Koi se yo otome*
> *Akaki kuchibiru Asenu ma ni*
> *Atsuki chishio no Hienu ma ni*
> *Asu no tsukihi wa Nai mono wo"*

(pg.36)

CHAPTER 1-3

The Writings of Kirima Seiichi – Seiichi's quotes are always a bit of a nightmare to translate, as they have to strike a balance between seeming cryptic but being vaguely understandable. Our translation is the result of studying the Japanese closely and puzzling out the meaning of the passages before ever translating a word. (pg.48)

CHAPTER 1-4

Did He or Didn't He? – Boogiepop says that he never appeared before the psychologist, but this is later contradicted in book six. (pg.54)

CHAPTER 2-1

The Village of Eight Graves – The first mystery novel starring famous fictional detective Kindaiichi Kousuke (referred to by some as the "Japanese Columbo"). Yokomizu Seishi's *The Village of Eight Graves* (or *Yatsuhaka Mura*) is a very fun book that is told in the grand tradition of adventure novels, such *as King Solomon's Mines,* in an overblooded, Victorian novel style. Apparently, it was inspired by the *Tsuyama Sanjuuninkoroshi* incident, in which thirty people were murdered. (pg.72)

Doctor Murder – Originally *"satsujin hakusei."* (pg.76)

CHAPTER 2-2

Karma Dance – An East Indian tribal dance that is performed during the worship of the God and Goddess of Fate—the bearers of good and bad fortune. The Japanese phrase would be *"karuma mai."* (pg.82)

CHAPTER 2-3

First Kitchen – A popular second-rate fast food chain in Japan. (pg. 89)

A Ready-Built House – Japanese people tend to buy a piece of land, knock down whatever house is on it, and have a new house built that is designed for their specific needs. It seems rare to actually live in a house that someone else has lived in. But at other times, real estate companies will build houses before they find buyers, like this one. (pg.91)

Note that Kirima Nagi's "brother," Taniguchi Masaki, is a central character in the next two books.

Ten-Mat Room – In Japan, *tatami* mats are used as units of measurement that tell you how large a room is. (pg.93)

Distortions of Reality – The word "*yugami*" can also be translated as "kinks" or "flaws," but we've chosen to go with the word "distortions," as the word will become a recurring motif that will be seen throughout the rest of the series—especially in the fifth novel, where it appears quite heavily. (pg.98)

CHAPTER 3-1

Being Scouted – The prep schools that scouted Yurihara seem to be regular high schools that are at a significantly higher level than Shinyo Academy. (pg. 116)

Diet Cola – This is actually left generic in Japanese. We can only assume that none of the major soft drink companies want themselves identified as having drinks that are good for dissolving fatal poison tablets in. (pg.117)

CHAPTER 4-1

Speech Patterns – Naoko's speech patterns change dramatically when she starts talking to Kimura. For that matter, so do Miyashita's a little later—something about him seems to make girls speak a bit more openly. Probably explains why he's got so many girlfriends.

MOS Burger – A fast-food restaurant chain that originated in Japan, and next to McDonald's, is the largest fast-food franchise in the country. (pg.153)

CHAPTER 4-2

Ronin – A student that failed his/her college entrance exams, and who is currently attending cram school. Keitaro Urashima from the series *Love Hina* is a prime example of a ronin. In feudal times, a ronin referred to a masterless samurai. (pg.157)

American Coffee – Coffee that is brewed weaker than a "regular" cup of coffee. (pg.158)

CHAPTER 4-3

Hoshi Shinichi – One of the most popular short story writers of Post-War Japan. During his career, Hoshi wrote over a thousand short stories and published several full-length novels and biographies. His area of special interest was in science fiction writing. (pg.162)

Tanabata Festival – Commonly known as "The Star Festival" and held on July 7th, this celebration is based on an ancient Chinese legend about an epic love story between the two stars Altair and Vega that are separated by the Milky Way, except for this one special day. (pg.162)

CHAPTER 5-2

Lecture Hall – Like an auditorium, but without chairs. (pg.189)

CHAPTER 5-3

You Aren't Human – Originally *"hitodenashi!"* This bit and the second reference to distortions in the world were by far the two most difficult lines in the book to translate, as it's difficult to try and capture the nuance of a line and still have it sound like something you'd shout at a moment like this. (pg.201)

Waiting Until Graduation – It does say a lot about the book's world view that Kei can't imagine Saotome Masami and the Manticore taking over the world until after they graduate. (pg.203)

CHAPTER 5-5

Rumors – Nagi's theory seems contradicted by Touka's reaction on the phone; she might be wrong. The *Boogiepop Dual* manga certainly suggests that the rumors about Boogiepop have been spread independently of Touka. (pg.216)

Join us now for a special sneak preview of
the second novel in the Boogiepop series.

Boogiepop
returns

written by
Kouhei Kadono

illustrated by
Kouji Ogata

english translation by
**Andrew
Cunningham**

Coming in
June 2006 from

Seven Seas

Prelude

On a very cold and snowy day in early March, a girl climbed to the top of our prefectural high school, Shinyo Academy, and proceeded to throw herself off of the roof of the building. Her name was Minahoshi Suiko. She was only seventeen.

"Mariko-san, what is it *you* like?" she asked me abruptly one day, back when she was still alive.

Without putting much thought into it, I gave her the name of a pop star that everyone was listening to.

"Hmm...really?"

"Yeah. He's kinda cool," I said offhandedly.

Suiko-san took a deep breath, faced the setting sun, and began to whistle.

Our school is up in the mountains, and it's a place where most students end up taking the bus to get to or from. On that particular day, Suiko-san and I had decided to walk home together, and we had the streets all to ourselves.

The tune she whistled turned out to be the most popular song of the pop star that I'd mentioned. It was clear from listening to her that she was an exceptional whistler. She made the melody seem quite beautiful, to the point that it sounded much, much better than the actual song itself. When she finished, I couldn't help but applaud.

"That was amazing! Suiko, you're really good!"

"Not really. If you liked it, it's because you already had a predisposition to liking it in the first place."

She was the type of person who said dramatic things like that, and it came to her quite naturally.

"You must have practiced, though. Do you play an instrument?"

"No, just by ear."

"Then you must have perfect pitch or something. That's awesome! What do you usually listen to?"

"Stuff nobody's ever heard of."

"Like what?"

"Mm, for example," and she took another breath, and began a different piece.

This time, it was more humming than whistling, as if she were a magical instrument that could reproduce any melody in existence.

"……!" I was so stunned just listening to her that I forgot to breathe.

There was simply no comparison to the first song. There was a resonance in my chest, a vibration in my heart that somehow made me feel very sad, all of a sudden. It was a strange melody—both rhythmical and powerful.

When she finished, I couldn't applaud. I was choked up, with tears welling up in my eyes.

"…What's wrong? Didn't you like it?"

"No…no! It was…it was…uh, I feel sort of embarrassed now. It's like my song was just an imitation of real music…"

"I thought you liked that song?"

"N-no, I think I couldn't have, really. When I heard your song just now, it felt like…this is the first time that I've ever really known that I liked a piece of music. And it didn't have anything to do with what's popular or trendy!" I cried, getting worked up.

"That's nice," Suiko-san said, smiling. She was as beautiful, if not more beautiful, than the song. And then, she stood there backlit by the red light of the evening sky. It was like I was seeing the silhouette of a goddess.

"What song was that?" I asked.

She giggled. "You won't laugh?"

"Why would I?"

"The name of the piece is *Salome*. It's from a ballet."

"What's odd about that?"

"The composer is Ifukube Akira."

"Who?"

"He's most famous for writing the soundtracks to monster movies," Suiko-san said, putting her hand to her mouth, shoulders trembling as she laughed.

This gesture was so feminine that it made my heart beat faster. I thought to myself that I could never laugh that naturally. No, there was nobody else I knew who could laugh so beautifully or as unreservedly as her.

But now she was no longer with us.

I couldn't understand it. Why would a girl like her ever want to kill herself?

They said she didn't leave a note. We don't know if she had some secret pain that drove her to it, or if she did it just to prove some kind of point.

But I wanted to know. I had to know.

I can't honestly say that the two of us were all that close.

But on those rare occasions where we were alone together, she would always talk to me. That was about it, though.

Still, she was without a doubt the most real person I'd ever met, up to that point. I can't think of any other way of describing it. Everyone else was just imitating someone else, trying desperately to pretend that it was their true nature. They were all frauds.

So I thought that there had to be some meaning behind her suicide.

That's why I'm going to follow her.

Is that imitation too? Probably.

What's sad is that I don't even know if I really loved her. And that's the irony; my life is going to end without me really understanding much of anything.

**

Komiya Mariko stood on the roof of the school, composing her suicide note in her head, but she decided not to write it down.

The sky was dark.

The sun had set a long time ago, and the last traces of light were quickly fading away.

"Suiko-san…"

She looked over the edge of the roof.

Below her, she could still see the white line where Minahoshi Suiko's body had landed. The world around her was almost completely dark, but that line alone seemed to glow, floating upwards.

She swallowed.

Something that Minahoshi Suiko had said to her once popped into her head.

"Mariko-san, there's nothing in this world that is truly decided. Birds sometimes fall out of the air, and sometimes it snows in April. Everything is uncertain, nothing is 'unnatural.'"

I wonder what that meant?

Perhaps I'll understand if I only climb over this fence…!

The white line moved, beckoning to her. It was an illusion, but it seemed too natural to call it that. It made perfect sense to Mariko.

There seemed to be no other logical choice of her doing anything else in life except jumping. The impulse rose up inside her. Her body shook, but not with fear—no, it was excitement.

"Suiko-san…!"

Komiya Mariko grabbed hold of the fence, preparing to climb.

But a voice came from behind her.

"—You wish to follow Minahoshi Suiko? You can't do it that way. It's impossible."

The voice was very strange…like that of a boy or a girl, yet at the same time, neither.

"——?!" Mariko turned around in surprise.

He sat on the other side of the roof, half hidden in darkness.

A pipe-shaped black hat half hid his eyes, and he was wrapped in a black cape with a number of rivets attached to it. There was black lipstick, contrasting with the white of his face.

"If you jump now, you will not end up where she has gone," he said quietly.

"Y-you're…?" Mariko said. She was clearly shaken, but not because she didn't know him. No, she knew all about him. All the girls in school were talking about him.

But for him to be real…?

"It seems you know me. That make things easier." His left eye narrowed, and the right side of his mouth curled up in a strange, asymmetrical expression.

"W-what do you mean? Why can't I go to her?"

"Simple. You are about to end your life of your own free will. But Minahoshi Suiko did not. If there is such a thing as heaven, you will surely end up in a different place than her." It would be accurate to describe his voice as chilly.

"She did not end her life of her 'own free will?' What does that mean?" Mariko felt as if the ground beneath her feet were crumbling.

"You know my name, don't you? Then you know what I do." He was half shrouded in darkness. It looked as if he were dissolving into thin air.

"Th-then…you?"

"Yes. I am a *shinigami*. Minahoshi Suiko did not kill herself. I…killed her."

"W-why?!"

"Because she was an enemy of the world."

"……!"

"So now what? Do you still wish to die? Unfortunately, I'm afraid I have no intention of killing you. You are not even worth that much."

"B-but…but…" Mariko stuttered, confused. She wasn't sure of anything now.

The enemy of the world? Suiko-san? How? What did that mean?

"Alternatively, I could put it this way. Minahoshi Suiko has not yet reached the next world. Unlike me, she was not 'divided,' but she was equally 'automatic.' But where she is now...I really couldn't tell you."

Mariko couldn't understand anything the cloaked figure was saying.

She hadn't reached the next world?

Reflexively, Mariko looked at the ground below on the other side of the fence. It was now too dark to make out the white line any longer.

It was crazy. Mariko had seen her...seen what used to be her, as the authorities carried her body away under a bloodstained, white shroud. What did it all mean?

"What does it mean, Boogie—?!" Mariko cried out, turning around...but the cloaked figure was gone.

She looked around, but came up with nothing. The darkness was too complete. It was impossible to tell where the mysterious figure in black had gone.

Or perhaps it had never physically been there at all.

"............"

At last, fear welled up in Mariko's heart.

She glanced at the ground below her.

But the fence that had seemed so easy to scale a moment ago now seemed as if it were a hundred meters tall.

"Aah..."

"It's impossible."
"You will not end up where she has gone."
"Minahoshi Suiko has not yet reached the next world."

Her legs shook.

"Aaaaah…!"

And Mariko crumbled, falling to the floor. Tear after tear rolled down her face. She couldn't stop them from coming. They were the first tears she'd shed since Minahoshi Suiko had died.

She had been convinced it was better to die than to cry, but now she couldn't hold the tears back.

"I'm sorry. I'm sorry…I'm sorry, I'm sorry, I'm sorry…" she whispered in a slow rhythm, as she rocked herself back and forth. But her tiny voice was faint and was swept away by the wind, and lost in the night.

***

"…………"

The figure in the black hat watched her from below. Beneath his feet was a white line in the shape of a person.

He went down on his knee, and ran his hand over the line.

"She's certainly not *here* any more…" he murmured, and stood up. "Are you going to try again? *Imaginator*?"

His black cape flapped furiously in the night wind.

1.

Sometimes I wake up in the middle of the night, she said. Her name was Nakadai Sawako, and her cheekbones stood out ever so slightly. But her face was very pale, and to Asukai Jin, she looked like a dried-up, withered bouquet inside an oversized jacket.

"Hmm," he said.

"I know it's cliché, but I feel like something's sitting on my chest, looking at me. But when I open my eyes…"

"There's nothing there?"

"Yes. I mean, I know it's a dream, but…I have it over and over again. So…"

Sawako's shoulders trembled. In her hair, there were still lingering traces of a two-month-old perm, but she wasn't one to take care of herself, and she had obviously paid little attention to it since then. And understandably so—there were only four more months left until the entrance exam. Like so many girls, she would make an appointment to have her hair straightened just before the big day, and then strive to take good care of it in order to make a good impression at the interview, but at the moment, she simply didn't have the time to care.

"This…'shadow'…" Asukai said, interrupting her. "Has it said anything to you?"

She looked up at him, surprised. "Yes! Yes, it has. How did you know?"

Ignoring her question, he asked another, "What did it say? Do you remember?"

"N-no, I…"

"You can't remember at all?"

"Right," she nodded.

The cram school was designed to squeeze a large number of people into a very small space to begin with, and the guidance office was hidden in a corner of the building. It was about the size of a prison's solitary confinement cell. And the two of them were all alone in the tiny room.

There was only one window—a long, thin, vertical slit in the wall, through which a single ray of light penetrated. The light was red. It was already evening.

"Hmm…" Asukai said again, shutting his mouth and looking down at the girl's chest.

'…She has no roots,' he thought. 'Very few leaves…only the buds are large, and they're almost breaking the stem…'

Sawako grew uncomfortable in the silence, and began locking her fingers together on her knees.

"Um, Asukai-sensei…?"

"…………" He didn't respond.

He had a pointed chin and a thin face with a serene beauty to it. He was not much older than Sawako, just past twenty. He was a student at a public university, but he taught art part time at this cram school. And he had taken over the highly unpopular position of guidance counselor.

"…………"

She looked up at him timidly. At some point, he'd taken his eyes off her and was staring out the window.

"I-I'm sorry, this all must sound crazy…" Sawako whispered, unable to stand it any longer.

Quietly, Asukai said, "As a teacher, I know I'm not supposed to say this. But maybe you should try not to take exams so seriously."

"What do you mean?"

"Getting into the best university isn't going to relieve you of your worries…or guarantee your future," he continued, almost like he was reading some inspirational pamphlet. "I know a lot of people who slaved away, got into college, and then had no idea what to do once they were there. All they'd ever done was study, and they didn't know how to just let go and enjoy themselves. So they'd go off to try and pass the civil servants exam or something. They were just pointlessly limiting their options for a…I dunno, a decent future. They meet the person they were supposed to fall in love with, but they don't recognize how valuable they would be, and without even noticing, they wind up missing out on the most important things in life.

"They're college students, but they can't shake the exam student mentality. And very few people can pass on their first try. Most people fail. They become *ronin*. They fritter away their precious youth, and end up, frankly, really screwed up because of it."

She just sat there listening, wide-eyed.

"You see?" Asukai asked, turning towards her.

"Um, not…"

"You *already know* this, don't you? But you're doing your very best *not to think about it*. But doing your best and avoiding the truth…they're two different things. We can't tell you not to overdo it, though. The only way to actually pass these tests…*is* to overdo it. But it's important not to burden you with excessive, and frankly, unrealistic expectations. I know you've heard this all before, but getting into college is not your whole life. That dream about the shadow is a sign that you're unconsciously resisting the notion of getting into college. I just think you need to relax a bit."

"O-okay," she nodded obediently. "But…but still…"

"Yeah. That's why you need to work at it. It isn't a bad thing to want to go to college. It's not like it's an impossible dream, either. But it just isn't healthy to get obsessed with it, you know? At this rate, you're just going to get overwhelmed by the pressure and be in no condition to actually sit there and take the test."

"I…I think I understand," Sawako said meekly.

'…The bud relaxed a little,' Asukai thought. 'If she could just make a few more leaves…not that it would take care of all of her problems, but it would be a start.'

He was looking at her chest again.

He could see something there.

Nobody else could see it, including the girl herself.

After that, they spoke in more concrete terms about how they should go about handling her problem subjects.

"—Thank you very much!" she yelled as she stood up twenty minutes later.

"Your effort is genuine. All you have to do is just stay calm, and keep moving forward."

"Okay. And thanks, Sensei," she started. "I feel much

better now. Say, did you ever have some sort of training? Like as a therapist or counselor?"

"Not really."

"Maybe you should consider a new career. You're really smart and good looking too." Asukai gave her an awkward smile, and she slapped her hand over her mouth. "Ah! Sorry! I didn't mean to be rude…!"

"I'll think about," he chuckled. "They do say you can't make a living painting."

As she was about to leave, Sawako suddenly turned back, remembering something. "Oh, right! Sensei, have you heard the phrase, 'Sometimes, it snows in April'?"

"What?" Asukai said, shocked.

"That's the only thing I remember from my dream. Oh, but it's probably not important. Good-bye!" she said brightly as she exited—her gloomy exterior having finally been shed.

"Sometimes…it snows in April?"

For some reason, those words made something stir inside Asukai.

***

When Asukai Jin thought about his strange ability to see the flaws in people's hearts, he always remembered Saint-Exupery's *The Little Prince*. He had read it when he was three or four years old, but he remembered one line from it that went something like, "The reason this child was beautiful was because he had a rose within his heart."

He felt as if that image had been carved into his psyche and left a lasting impression on him.

His eyes could see a single plant growing from every

person's chest. The variety of plant in his vision varied, and they came in all sorts of shapes and sizes, but the problem was not the variety of plant, but with the very fact that in every vision, there was some part missing.

Perhaps there was no flower. Or no leaves. No stem. Or, like this girl, no roots. He had never once seen a person that carried a complete plant within their chest.

There was always a flaw.

So, his 'advice' was simply to say whatever was needed to compensate for that flaw. If there were no roots, all he had to do was tell them to have more confidence. Everyone would be satisfied by that, and recover their good cheer.

His job at the cram school finished, he walked back to his apartment along a bustling shopping street. He couldn't help but notice the flaws on everyone's chests.

It annoyed him, occasionally.

Human effort was entirely devoted to making up for this flaw. He knew this. But he also knew that what they lacked was never in them to begin with, and it was something that could never be obtained.

He had looked at his own chest before, but he could find nothing there. Presumably, he was lacking something also, and it was that missing item that was making him so unhappy. Unfortunately, there was no way for him to replace it either.

"…So that's why *I* said…"

"…What the…?"

"…Hahaha! That's so *dumb*…"

Drunks, young people, old people, males, females…they all passed him by. None of them ever thought that they were missing flowers or roots.

(They're happier *not* knowing…)

Since he was very young, he had always felt isolated.

Perhaps he always would.

"—Oh, look! Snow!"

"Wow! It's so pretty!"

Everyone around him was cheering at the sky, so Asukai felt obligated look up as well.

Something white was falling out of the night sky.

(I do like snow…)

Snow turned everything white. It was one of his favorite things. Perhaps because flowers never bloomed beneath it. He could go about his business without thinking about anything else…or so he felt.

But when he looked happily up at the sky, his expression suddenly froze.

There was a girl standing in the fifth story window of a nearby building.

Her feet were on the window ledge, her body all the way outside, getting ready to jump.

As he stared up at her, their eyes met.

She smiled slightly with her eyes. Then…

"No…!" Asukai tried to shout, but she flung her body outward into the open air.

Reflexively, Asukai ran towards her.

But his feet went out from under him, and he fell awkwardly.

He hurriedly scrambled back to his feet, but as looked up again, he saw something impossible.

"Heh heh heh."

The girl was floating in mid-air, laughing.

But there was something unique about her smile. Her mouth was closed in a straight line, and her eyes alone smiled, sweet and enchanting.

She was frozen in mid-air, about to fall, but not moving at all.

"Hunh…?" he wondered.

"Hey, wake up! You're in the way," snarled a group of drunks, brushing past him.

"D-do you see that?" Asukai asked, pointing at the girl.

None of them paid much attention. "What are you on about?"

"You've had too much to drink!"

They were looking where he was pointing, but none of them could see her.

(W-what on earth…?)

He stood up, looking up at her, stunned.

Now that he looked carefully, he could tell that she was actually falling, just very, very slowly. Her tangled hair was moving, swaying.

"Heheheh."

Those laughing eyes drank in the light like they were holes in the sky.

"It isn't much fun to see things nobody else can, is it, Asukai-sensei?" he heard her whisper in his ear.

"How…?"

"I know exactly how you feel. I used to be the same."

Asukai stumbled over, until he was directly below the falling girl.

"Th-then you…"

"Just like your extra sensory perception, I can see people's deaths."

Her expression never changed—that tightly closed mouth never moved. It was as if time around her moved at a snail's pace.

"Deaths?"

"To be more accurate, I can see the energy field generated by all living things just before they burn themselves out." She laughed again. "I represent a possibility, in which people are able to manipulate death. My purpose is to recreate the world in that fashion, which makes me an enemy of the current world. Even in spring, I bring cold. I make it snow in April."

"Er…"

"Will you help me with my work, Asukai-sensei?"

"What…? What are you talking about? Who are you?!" he shouted.

The people around him looked at him suspiciously. To them, he was shouting at empty space. They must have thought him plastered beyond his limit or tripped out on drugs.

In the air above him, the girl replied, "My enemies call me the *Imaginator*."

And she vanished.

"W-wait!" he cried, reaching out towards her, but his fingers only brushed empty space.

"…………."

He was astounded, but then his shoulders slumped in disappointment. He thought to himself that he had finally gone completely insane. Seeing things. It was obvious—and then he glanced at his feet, and almost shouted.

The falling snow had piled up all around, except at his feet, where a small patch of pavement was left exposed.

It was like a shadow puppet in the shape of a girl falling from the sky.

To be continued in

Boogiepop returns

Coming in June 2006

The hit novel becomes
the must-have manga...

Boogiepop
doesn't laugh

Volume 1 Coming April 2006

Seven Seas

About the Author

Born in 1968, Kouhei Kadono grew up uncertain about his direction in life. He spent a considerable portion of his early years frittering away his youth before somehow ending up writing novels.

In 1997, Kadono-sensei's first *Boogiepop* novel, *Boogiepop and Others*, took First Place in the Media Works' Dengeki Game Novel Contest. Early the following year, the novel was released to widespread acclaim and ignited the Japanese "light novel" (young adult) trend. Since that time, Kadono-sensei has written thirteen *Boogiepop* novels and several related works such as the *Beat's Discipline* short story collections and the two *Boogiepop* manga series entitled *Boogiepop Doesn't Laugh* and *Boogiepop Dual*. In its entirety, the *Boogiepop* series has seen over two million copies in print and spawned a live action movie and a hit anime series.

In addition to the *Boogiepop* universe, Kadono-sensei's body of literary work includes a wide array of fantasy and mystery novels such as the *Jiken, Soul Drop, Limited World* and *Night Watch* series.

About the Illustrator

Born in 1970, a native of Osaka, Kouji Ogata spent his early twenties struggling to get enough credits to graduate from Osaka Design School. In late 1996, Ogata-sensei was commissioned by Media Works to illustrate the first *Boogiepop* novel, *Boogiepop and Others*.

At the time, Ogata-sensei was simply a rising star with a distinctive, eye-catching art style, but he gradually was able to further hone his artistic skills with each subsequent work. His watercolor-style paneling seen in the two-volume *Boogiepop Doesn't Laugh* manga series was a particularly high point of his early career.

In addition to providing illustrations for novels and manga, Ogata-sensei has been involved with supplying character designs for anime productions including *Boogiepop Phantom, Spirit* and *Gin-iro no kami no Agito*.

In his free time he enjoys motorcycles, tennis, and remote controlled models.